MONUMENTAL JESUS

Midcentury: Architecture, Landscape, Urbanism, and Design
Richard Longstreth, Editor

# MONUMENTAL JESUS

Landscapes of Faith and Doubt in Modern America

Margaret M. Grubiak

University of Virginia Press

CHARLOTTESVILLE AND LONDON

University of Virginia Press

© 2020 by the Rector and Visitors of the University of Virginia

All rights reserved

Printed in the United States of America on acid-free paper

*First published 2020*

9  8  7  6  5  4  3  2  1

Library of Congress Cataloging-in-Publication Data

Names: Grubiak, Margaret M., author.

Title: Monumental Jesus : landscapes of faith and doubt in modern America / Margaret M. Grubiak.

Description: Charlottesville : University of Virginia Press, 2020. | Series: Midcentury : architecture, landscape, urbanism, and design | Includes bibliographical references and index.

Identifiers: LCCN 2019036808 (print) | LCCN 2019036809 (ebook) | ISBN 9780813943749 (cloth) | ISBN 9780813943756 (ebook)

Subjects: LCSH: Christianity and culture—United States. | Cultural landscapes—United States. | Popular culture—Religious aspects—Christianity. | United States—Religion.

Classification: LCC BR115.C8 .G759 2020 (print) | LCC BR115.C8 (ebook) | DDC 306.6/773—dc23

*LC record available at https://lccn.loc.gov/2019036808*

*LC ebook record available at https://lccn.loc.gov/2019036809*

Portions of chapters 1 and 3 previously appeared in "Visualizing the Modern Catholic University: The Original Intention of 'Touchdown Jesus' at the University of Notre Dame," *Material Religion* 6, no. 3 (November 2010): 336–68, and in "An Architecture for the Electronic Church: Oral Roberts University in Tulsa, Oklahoma," *Technology and Culture* 57, no. 2 (April 2016): 380–413.

Cover art: *Christ of the Ozarks* statue (1966), sculptor Emmet Sullivan, Eureka Springs, Arkansas (RosaIreneBetancourt 12/Alamy Stock Photo)

*For Joe and Mary Anne Grubiak,*
*For the gift of faith*

*For Michael,*
*Always*

*The eleven disciples went to Galilee, to the mountain to which Jesus had ordered them. When they saw him, they worshipped, but they doubted.*

—MATTHEW 28:16–17

# CONTENTS

# ILLUSTRATIONS

# PREFACE

I am a person of faith, but I am also a person of doubt. I am Catholic, and yet my personal liturgical year swings wildly from skepticism about the sinless state of the Blessed Virgin Mary celebrated on the Solemnity of the Immaculate Conception to my complete and utter conviction of our eternal salvation narrated in the powerfully moving Easter Triduum services. There are times when I question how I can consider myself Catholic when I struggle with some of the central tenets of my faith, but other times when I am absolutely affirmed in my religious beliefs.

I am far from the only person to possess religious doubt, nor am I the only person to hold complex and at times contradictory views on my personal religion. For many of us, the matrix of our personal religious belief—or absence thereof—is a constant reworking and challenging of belief. How we go about doing this is the focus of this book. I teach at a university associated with my faith, where my classes put me in touch with some of the most important writings of my religion, and my generous colleagues with specialties in theology and philosophy offer a wellspring of resources. And yet how I actually confront the real issues of my faith is not primarily in these literary experiences or high-minded circles. What makes me awake to the central questions of my faith is the everyday encounter with religion as I go about my daily life. Our environments are saturated with religion and statements of faith, from the visible steeples in our neighborhoods, to the ringing of church bells, to the Star of David necklace on the stranger we pass, to the Christian symbol of the fish on the car in front of us, to the highway billboard imploring us to accept Jesus in order to be saved.

These moments of seeing religion in our everyday life are moments in which we confront questions of belief. And the ways that we respond—with gentle humor, with caustic satire, with outright blasphemy—are remarkable. We bring to these sincere constructions of faith a framework of the world infused with popular culture that seems to be at odds with religion, and yet the responses to faith we generate through this framework are revealing and fascinating. These responses are the focus of this book. We construct landscapes of doubt, of questioning and challenge, in response to landscapes of faith that make questions about religion very real and present to our everyday world. Landscapes of doubt are of a piece with landscapes of faith, but landscapes of doubt make us see religious architecture and images in a different way, from the viewpoint of doubter rather than believer. And in this posture of doubt, religion is never more alive.

Like many authors, I have had the good fortune of being cheered on in this work by generous colleagues. I am particularly grateful for support from James Bielo, Lydia Mattice Brandt, Steven Cornell, Michael Crosbie, Philip Herrington, Catherine Kahl Miliaras, Elizabeth Milnarik, Timothy Kent Parker, Catherine Osborne, Karen Robbins, and Susan and Bill Trollinger. My thinking on this topic has been greatly shaped by conversations with Karla Britton, Jeanne Halgren Kilde, Colleen McDannell, and David Morgan, and I am especially grateful to Gretchen Buggeln, who helped me to rethink this work from its early form. I thank Anat Geva for her encouragement on publication. I was also able to work on this book's ideas in presentations at meetings of the Society of Architectural Historians; the Latrobe Chapter of the Society of Architectural Historians; the Southeast Chapter of the Society of Architectural Historians; the American Academy of Religion; and the Architecture, Culture, and Spirituality Forum. I am grateful for the feedback in each of these settings, especially for those who challenged this book's arguments. While any faults of this book are mine alone, I am indebted for my approach to architectural history and material religion to my professors Richard Guy Wilson, Daniel Bluestone, Louis Nelson, and Dell Upton from my time in the University of Virginia's Department of Architectural History.

For their encouragement and suggestions, I deeply thank my colleagues in the Department of Humanities at Villanova University. Discussions with my students in my Architecture and Religion in America course helped shape these ideas as well, and to these students I am grateful. Much of this book was written while on sabbatical from Villanova University, which provided further financial support via the Villanova University Subvention of Publication Program and a VERITAS Faculty Research Program grant. I am grateful to the Villanova community for giving me the time, space, and support to explore this subject.

Given the sensitive nature of the humor and satire of religion this book engages, I would like to thank those institutions that have engaged with this work and helped me clarify my writing on their beliefs. I am particularly grateful to The Church of Jesus Christ of Latter-day Saints, especially Anne Berryhill and Emily Utt, for assistance and clarifications.

For their assistance in obtaining images, I thank Charles Lamb and Peter Lysy at the University of Notre Dame University Archives; Linda Lynn at *The Oklahoman;* Richard Aldacushion at the *Washington Post;* Katie Duncan at *Deseret News;* the New York Public Library Manuscripts and Archives Division; Special Collections at the University of Washington Libraries; Sheri Perkins of the Tulsa City-County Library; the San Francisco Theological Seminary Library; Raegan Carmona of Andrews McMeel Syndication; Jane Freedman; Tricia Gesner of the Associated Press; and Cordesia Pope and Jutta Seibert at Villanova University's Falvey Memorial Library. My gratitude goes to those institutions that granted permission to publish images.

I have previously published parts of this book in academic journals. Portions of chapter 1, "Touchdown Jesus!," appeared in Margaret M. Grubiak, "Visualizing the Modern Catholic University: The Original Intention of 'Touchdown Jesus' at the University of Notre Dame," *Material Religion* 6, no. 3 (November 2010): 336–68. Portions of chapter 3, "Adventures in the Evangelical Theme Park," previously appeared in Margaret M. Grubiak, "An Architecture for the Electronic Church: Oral Roberts University in Tulsa, Oklahoma," *Technology and Culture* 57, no. 2

(April 2016): 380–413. I am grateful to S. Brent Plate at *Material Religion,* Barbara Hahn and Suzanne Moon at *Technology and Culture,* and the anonymous peer reviewers who helped shape this research and writing in these early settings.

I also thank the anonymous reviewers of this book's manuscript for their comments that profoundly recast this book, and the editors at the University of Virginia Press, especially acquisitions editor Boyd Zenner and series editor Richard Longstreth, for giving this book's perspective a venue to be heard.

Finally, and most importantly, I thank my parents, Joe and Mary Anne Grubiak, for their encouragement, and especially to my father for reading chapters and asking me "How is the book coming along?" as a way to lift my spirits in the long book-writing process. My knowledge of the places, buildings, and images I discuss here comes largely from my adventures with my husband, Michael Tran, whose willingness to travel with me and explore architecture is something for which I am eternally grateful.

PREFACE

MONUMENTAL JESUS

# INTRODUCTION

On May 25, 1980, at 7:00 p.m., televangelist Oral Roberts saw the extraordinary: a 900-foot Jesus appeared to him in a vision. Jesus assured Roberts that the City of Faith, a $120 million trio of skyscrapers then under construction at Oral Roberts University in Tulsa, Oklahoma, would be completed through generous donations from Roberts's prayer partners. As Jesus said to Roberts, "I told you when I chose you to build it that you couldn't build it by yourself, but that I would speak to your partners and through them I WOULD BUILD IT."[1] In a newsletter appeal to these prayer partners, Roberts recounted his vision:

> I felt an overwhelming holy presence all around me. When I opened my eyes, there He stood ... some 900 feet tall, looking at me ... He stood a full 300 feet taller than the 600 foot tall City of Faith. There I was face to face with Jesus Christ, the Son of the Living God ... He stared at me without saying a word; Oh! I will never forget those eyes! And then, He reached down, put His hands under the City of Faith, lifted it, and said to me, "See how easy it is for Me to lift it!"[2]

A drawing of the 900-foot Jesus lifting up the City of Faith that accompanied appeals for donations further transformed this vision from individual to communal witness.[3] These verbal and visual accounts testified that God and Jesus were present to us now on Earth, in our modern age, and could make miraculous things happen. Jesus's words to Oral Roberts were indeed prophetic. Nearly $5 million came in from half a million contributors to help finish the construction of the City of Faith, opened in 1981 to house a hospital, clinic, and medical research facility that combined modern medicine with faith healing. The 60-foot bronze statue of *The Healing Hands* Roberts commissioned for the base of the towers made visible, in part, the corporeality of the 900-foot Jesus in this landscape of faith (see fig. 22).

Yet Roberts's vision of a 900-foot Jesus was also met with doubt. Fellow preachers publicly denounced Roberts's vision as a lie.[4] While Roberts would later say in an 1982 interview with talk show host Phil Donahue that he did not see Jesus with his physical eyes but rather with his inner eyes (a distinction he made also at the dedication of the City of Faith in 1981), at the time of his appeal for donations, Roberts asserted that he had literally seen a 900-foot Jesus.[5] The popular and national press seized on the extraordinary claim of seeing Jesus Christ standing at 900 feet tall, an image ripe for humor, satire, and ridicule. As Oral Roberts biographer David Edwin Harrell Jr. summarized various accounts, it was the scale of Jesus that captured people's imaginations: they mused about the amount of Visine required for a 900-foot Jesus's eyes, the size of a 900-foot Jesus's shoes, and the need for a 2,000-foot cross for a 900-foot Jesus.[6] An article in the *Christian Century,* a major Protestant publication, questioned the credibility of a 900-foot Jesus in a satiric mathematical investigation.[7] The apparent outrageousness of Oral Roberts's claim inspired the stage name of American rapper and musician Mark Griffin: MC 900 Ft. Jesus.[8] Even if Christians and others could accept the humanity of Jesus—that he had a human body, at human scale, and felt pain, hunger, exhaustion, and pleasure just as we do—it seemed that the idea of a supersized Jesus walking around Earth (in Tulsa, no less) was a bridge too far.

One altered photograph satirizing Roberts's vision vividly placed the 900-foot Jesus within a landscape of doubt (fig. 1). With the City of Faith buildings in the background, a doctored sign near the center of the photograph reads "BEGIN 900 FT. JESUS X-ING" with an image of a praying Jesus in silhouette. The sign's

**Figure 1.** Altered photograph of Oral Roberts University's City of Faith satirizing Oral Roberts's religious vision of a 900-foot Jesus. ("A Cross to Bear," *Saturday Oklahoman and Times* [Oklahoma City], December 19, 1981, 19)

words and image played on government-issued road signs, co-opting their authority and seriousness. Yet rather than alerting us to animals crossing the road, the sign calls us instead to watch out for a 900-foot Jesus, described as such in the words "900 FT. JESUS" and in the black silhouette of a man dressed in long robes, with a beard, his head tilted upward toward heaven and his hands grasped in the gesture of prayer. Because we understand the sign to be official by analogy to others we regularly see, at first glance of the image we are lured into accepting the presence of a 900-foot Jesus before we process it as incongruous and therefore funny. This altered photograph wittily situates an image of the 900-foot Jesus in the actual landscape of the City of Faith and Oral Roberts University. In viewing the altered photograph—made into a poster for sale locally in Tulsa for six dollars in 1981 and reproduced by the Associated Press with an explanatory caption that ran in the *Saturday Oklahoman and Times* newspaper—we are simultaneously made part of the witnessing of Oral Roberts's vision and the humorous and even satirical response to it.[9]

These images of the 900-foot Jesus introduce us to landscapes of faith and doubt in modern America mediated by the built environment. The drawing of the 900-foot Jesus lifting up the City of Faith buildings made Roberts's vision explicit to spur his prayer partners to donate money, and the ultimate completion of the City of Faith buildings seemed to affirm this faith in religious visions and the belief that God can make great things happen (though the closing of the City of Faith only eight years later due to bankruptcy challenged this affirmation). This was a landscape of faith. The altered photograph of the 900-foot Jesus crossing created an alternative landscape of doubt. The idea that a 900-foot Jesus could appear at any moment in the vicinity of the City of Faith buildings seemed laughable to some. The anonymous generator of the poster, those who purchased it, and those who saw the image and responded to its humor countered the faith of Oral Roberts and his followers. For them, the idea that Jesus could be physically present to us in our modern world was ridiculous, and Oral Roberts's supposed religious vision was a mere scam for money for those foolish enough to believe. These landscapes of faith and doubt cast the meaning of religious architecture and image in profoundly different ways.

The visible responses to religious faith help us see religious architecture differently. Most often, we focus on the believer when it comes to religious architecture—those who construct these buildings and those who enact faith through ritual and community membership in their use. This book proposes an alternative focus on the reception of religious buildings by those who are not believers, those who are involuntarily confronted by religious buildings in the course of daily life, and those believers who have doubts. I am specifically concerned here with reactions (humor, satire, ridicule, blasphemy) that challenge these landscapes of faith in forms that make doubt visible (graffiti, altered photographs, cartoons, nicknames). These reactions destabilize and recast the meaning of religious buildings and images, as the examples in this book show. The nickname "Touchdown Jesus" transforms *The Word of Life* mural on the library at the University of Notre Dame into an image of Jesus as a football referee. The graffiti "SURRENDER DOROTHY" recasts the Mormon temple outside of Washington, D.C., into the Palace of Oz from *The Wizard of Oz*. The Reverend Jerry Falwell imagined a split screen with his plunge down the waterslide at Jim and Tammy Faye Bakker's Heritage USA religious theme park, immortalized in a photograph by the Associated Press beamed around the world, juxtaposed against an image of Pope John Paul II's arrival in Miami for an official state visit that very same day. An episode of *The Simpsons* co-opted Heritage USA to question the Pentecostal tenet of religious visions. As we have seen, the doctored photograph of Oral Roberts's City of Faith put the 900-foot Jesus in the landscape of the real, and a *Doonesbury* cartoon transformed another Oral Roberts claim into a ridicule of televangelism. A *MAD* magazine parody of "Charles Darwin's Night at the Creation Museum" undercut the Young Earth creationist belief manifested in the Creation Museum and Ark Encounter in Kentucky. Finally, reported threats to blow up the *Christ of the Ozarks* statue in Eureka Springs, Arkansas, reveal a complicated landscape of faith and hatred. Landscapes of doubt arise from landscapes of faith—they are cut from the same cloth—but landscapes of doubt illuminate questions about religion and faith in new and more often startling ways.

Doubt in this book means more than simply denial or rejection of faith, though certainly this closing off is part of our examples here. Doubt here also means questioning, challenging, investigation, ambiguity, and the possibility of belief, and it can be a key component to accepting religious faith as much as it can be about rejecting it. Doubt can be about the nature of religious institutions as well as the central tenants of faith. The examples in this book bear questions related to both. Can prayer really be used to secure victory in a football game? Is the Mormon faith a fraud? Is it OK for preachers to earn large sums of money for themselves as they raise money for their ministries? Can religion and the sacred be found in our leisure and entertainment time? What do I believe about the creation of humans and the world? How can someone claim Christian membership while holding hate-filled beliefs? Can a 900-foot Jesus possibly be real? This book argues that landscapes of doubt generated by people's responses to religious architecture and image are just as important as the positive affirmation of faith we see in religious architecture and image, or landscapes of faith. Landscapes of doubt—funny, sharp, caustic, blasphemous—reawaken us to fundamental questions about faith.

## Reimagining Religious Architecture

Religious buildings are constructed with clear purpose: they gather faith communities, house ritual, educate, and proselytize. Their size, materiality, decoration, and architectural style embody and communicate religious identity and religious belief. And yet all this intentionality and money invested cannot fully secure how they will be received. Religious buildings can also be ignored, misinterpreted, and acted against. As architectural historian Dell Upton has written about the unpredictability of architecture's reception, "the landscape, ostensibly the object of intention, ricochets back on us in unexpected ways. Most of what is important about architecture is *un*intended." In this view, the significance of the landscape is "created more by construing than by construction."[10] Upton theorized a "cultural landscape" that is "the fusion of the physical with the imaginative structures that all inhabitants of the landscape use in constructing and construing it," riveting our attention on the reception of architecture and landscape by a wider public. Upton advocated for understanding the many ways in which buildings are perceived: "Since there can be no normative perception, the human environment is necessarily the product of powerful yet diffuse imaginations, fractured by the faultlines of class, culture, and personality. It cannot be universalized, canonized, or even unified."[11] When we apply Upton's cultural landscape theory to religious landscapes that include religious architecture and images, we understand the many ways that faith and doubt are shaped not just by the institutions and people who construct religious buildings but also by those outsiders (and insiders) who construe new meanings for them.[12] In this book, landscapes of faith mean the positive assertion of faith found in religious buildings, while landscapes of doubt are the imaginative, visual responses to religious buildings that complicate their meaning. Landscapes of doubt—the true complement of landscapes of faith—are dynamic places in the exploration, deconstruction, and reconstruction of religious belief.

How people go about construing religion when they encounter religious architecture and images is the key focus of this book. Understanding what people *do* with religious images and objects has been the topic of religious visual and material culture scholars including David Morgan, Sally Promey, Colleen McDannell, and Gretchen Buggeln.[13] Morgan's concept of visual piety, or "the constructive operation of seeing that looks for, makes room for, the transcendent in daily life," highlights the active construction of meaning through the "sacred gaze."[14] As Colleen McDannell argues in her foundational book *Material Christianity,* material religion is important because it is an active agent in our practicing of religion: "Experiencing the physical dimensions of religion helps *bring about* religious values, norms, behaviors, and attitudes."[15] I am interested in the ways that people actively engage with the religious built environment by reimagining it—challenging it, remixing it, questioning it—in forms that take on the visible. This participatory response is a powerful method of engagement with the built environment and with religion. In proposing a reception theory for architecture, Cristina Garduño Freeman recalls culture scholar Henry Jenkins's idea of "participatory culture" that "posits the individuals of an audience as 'active, critically engaged and creative' members of society. They appropriate, transform, and extend objects of mass culture value as creative expressions and forms of civic engagement."[16] The religious architecture and images in this book are highly visible objects that possess such a mass culture value. The creative acts toward them—witty nicknames, doctored photographs, cartoon parodies—visualize an alternative world of religious meaning that may not bring about religious values in the affirmative way that McDannell means or make room for the transcendent in the way that Morgan intends, but they activate an invigorated engagement with religion through questioning and challenge.

Popular culture is a powerful medium by which people relate to and reimagine religion and religious buildings. Drivers on Washington, D.C.'s Capital Beltway see the Mormon temple as something from *The Wizard of Oz*. Football fans at the University of Notre Dame understand the mural visible over the stadium as part of football culture. Jim Bakker himself cultivated the comparison of Heritage USA to Disneyland and Disney World. Oral Roberts could not resist the powerful, futuristic imagery of the 1962 Seattle World's Fair as inspiration for his own university campus. Viewers of *The Simpsons* know Homer's evangelical neighbor Ned Flanders in part by his connection to Oral Roberts University, and *MAD* magazine satirized the Creation Museum through a parody of the promotional poster for the 2006 movie *Night at the Museum*. In framing religious architecture through the lens of popular culture—movies, sports, theme parks, world's fairs, and television—these buildings are made intelligible to a wider audience, and critiques of them within this popular culture frame find wider resonance.[17] Religion and popular culture's reciprocal relationship also works in the other direction when we apply a religious frame to popular culture. Erika Doss, Kathryn Lofton, and Michael Novak have explored this phenomenon in their respective studies of the religious overtones of Elvis culture, Oprah, and sports, and David Chidester has also considered the intermingling of religion and popular culture in America.[18] The fluid interplay between religion and popular culture—understanding religion within popular culture, and seeing popular culture through the lens of religion—extends to our built and visual environments.

These popular culture responses to religious buildings and images are deeply intertwined with mass culture and mass media. Millions encounter "Touchdown Jesus" via televised Notre Dame home football games. Satires of religious buildings created in cartoons and photographs are transmitted via newspapers and the internet. *Doonesbury's* "Death Watch" of Oral Roberts in his Prayer Tower at Oral Roberts University ran in newspapers nationally and internationally in 1987, and the Associated Press photograph of Jerry Falwell descending the waterslide at the Heritage USA theme park not only appeared widely in newspapers in 1987 but is also now enshrined on the Wikipedia webpage for Heritage USA as a significant historical artifact.[19] The witnessing of the Washington D.C. Mormon Temple in the context of *The Wizard of Oz* is made possible by another kind of mass culture— automobile culture—where the windshield becomes another screen through which we see the world. The transmission of these reimagined religious landscapes through mass media and culture—television, newspapers, magazines, print media, car culture—adds another dimension to how architectural meaning is remade and transmitted, just as Beatriz Colomina explored the relationship of modern architecture and mass media, and it widens the circle of those who are actively remaking religious meaning.[20] So, for example, not only is the anonymous graffiti artist who scrawls "SURRENDER DOROTHY" in sight of the Mormon temple an active remaker of the building's meaning, but so too is everyone who reads the graffiti and laughs at it. As Naomi Stead and Cristina Garduño Freeman have claimed, "Today, in a contemporary media environment of 'producers' and interactive participatory culture, media audiences are likely to be considered to be active agents in making, appropriating, and remixing media and culture, and thus in remaking it anew."[21]

Threaded through these reimaginings of religious architecture in popular culture and mass media is the use of humor, satire, ridicule, and blasphemy to challenge and transform religious meaning. Whereas religious humor operates as lighthearted and insightful, religious satire treads on the judgmental, hurtful, and even blasphemous while combating corruption and hypocrisy and challenging religious tenets. Religious humor, satire, and blasphemy have long literary and oral traditions, and their insights and critiques also are made visible in art, cartoons, media, and architecture.[22] S. Brent Plate's examination of blasphemous religious art makes explicit the powerful and often uncomfortable reframing of religion that is "obscene, impious, idolatrous, offensive, subversive and taboo," and David Morgan has studied the destruction of statues deemed idolatrous.[23] But missing from our exploration of the religious built environment specifically is how humor, satire, and blasphemy—from the benign to the hurtful—reframe how these buildings mean.[24] Religious humor and satire, along with popular culture and mass media, are powerful ways by which people respond to the religious architecture and images they encounter in their landscapes. They are the methods of constructing landscapes of doubt.

## Insiders and Outsiders, Believers and Doubters

Landscapes of doubt share commonalities in their roots in humor and satire, popular culture, and mass media, but how their meaning is construed by people inside a faith and outside of it is far from uniform.[25] Landscapes of doubt differ from landscapes of faith, whose audiences have clearer distinctions. We can identify the producer of a religious building as the religious institution or denomination and the user as the congregation. They constitute religious insiders who know intimately their religious building as a church home and setting for ritual and community. Those who are not members of the congregation, who never enter the building or use it, are outsiders. They may encounter a religious building in the course of their daily patterns of travel, and they may understand some of its religious symbolism, but for these outsiders the building is not an embedded part of their spiritual life. For landscapes of faith, insiders and outsiders have clearer margins.

For landscapes of doubt, by contrast, the audiences of religious buildings are complex and overlapping, constituting insiders and outsiders, believers and doubters, and people in between. Those who generate landscapes of doubt can be insiders and outsiders; they can gently poke fun to get at truths or harshly attack to declare untruths. Those who react to landscapes of doubt—insiders and outsiders—can be entertained or offended, or both at once; they can perceive landscapes of doubt as opportunities for reflection or as entirely hostile acts. The chapters in this book explore these varied dimensions of landscapes of doubt. While the concept of landscapes of faith and doubt can be applied to many religions, cultures, and time periods, I offer here Christian examples in the United States from the 1960s to today, chosen for the ways they assert belief through religious architecture and image and how people have reacted to them in ways that take on visual form.

Chapter 1 considers how the renaming of the thirteen-story *Word of Life* mural on the University of Notre Dame's skyscraper library as "Touchdown Jesus" transforms how we see and understand the mural. The nickname arose from the vernacular, most likely by Catholic insiders, as a funny, witty expression of Notre Dame culture, and both Catholic insiders and outsiders embrace the name. Father Theodore Hesburgh, the president of the University of Notre Dame at the time of the mural's construction, characterized "Touchdown Jesus" as "a nice, friendly, familiar name for this beautiful piece of art."[26] "Touchdown Jesus" is a memorable name that provokes a smile, but it also conjures a set of serious questions about the meaning of prayer and the uses of religion. "Touchdown Jesus" is an example of a landscape of doubt—of questioning—that while coming from the inside with gentle humor nevertheless raises questions about belief.

By contrast, the reframing of the Mormon temple outside of Washington, D.C., as something from *The Wizard of Oz,* the focus of chapter 2, was the act of outsiders and, while humorous on the surface, possesses hostile undertones. The temple's dramatic siting on the Washington, D.C., Beltway combined with the building's castellated architecture recall an image of the Emerald City from the movie, prompting a decades-long tradition of the graffiti "SURRENDER DOROTHY" scrawled on a railroad bridge in front of the building in an act of unsanctioned renaming. Such an alignment made a paradoxically highly visible but largely inaccessible building (open only to "temple worthy" Mormons) intelligible through a widely known popular culture icon and story. While this alignment of the temple with a popular culture icon at first appears simply wry and witty, the reframing also suggests that the Mormon faith is fraudulent, much like the Wizard of Oz was revealed to be the man behind the curtain perpetuating the fraud of the great and terrible Oz. Mormons know of and are aware of the graffiti, and much like their reaction to the highly satirical and blasphemous *The Book of Mormon* Broadway musical, where The Church of Jesus Christ of Latter-day Saints (LDS Church) advertised in the playbill, the response of the LDS Church has been to acknowledge the graffiti as an opportunity for outreach and missionary activity. "When they don't know you, people seem to think you resemble Oz," one temple administrator said. "That's why we have a visitor's [sic] center."[27] For the Mormon temple, a landscape of faith is transformed into a landscape of doubt by outsider renaming, raising questions about the exclusivity of Mormonism and the very foundation of its faith, but also prompting the opportunity for education about that very faith.

For Pentecostal televangelists Jim and Tammy Faye Bakker and Oral Roberts, their landscapes of faith—the Heritage USA theme park and Oral Roberts University—were recast into landscapes of doubt by both outsiders and some insiders who questioned the validity of religious visions and televangelist fundraising methods. The long-running satirical sitcom *The Simpsons* patterned evangelical neighbor Ned Flanders's Praiseland theme park on Heritage USA, using the park to argue religious visions are a fraud caused by a gas leak rather than a true spiritual experience, while also denigrating the evangelical theme park's marrying of religion and entertainment. The Associated Press photograph of the Reverend Jerry Falwell falling down Heritage USA's waterslide was transformed into a satirical image by Falwell himself, who contrasted the ridiculousness of the fundraising stunt with the dignified image of Pope John Paul II's arrival in the United States for an official state visit the same day. As we have already seen, the altered photograph of Oral Roberts University to include a 900-foot Jesus crossing sign ridiculed Roberts's spiritual vision, a key Pentecostal belief. And when Oral Roberts claimed "God will call me home" if his prayer partners failed to donate money to keep the City of Faith from bankruptcy, cartoonist Garry Trudeau set up an Oral Roberts "Death Watch" in his *Doonesbury* comic strip. As chapter 3 explores, the Pentecostal belief in the supernatural presence in our world and televangelical co-opting of popular culture for religion became flashpoints for the generation of these landscapes of doubt.

In chapter 4, we see a highly combative exchange between landscapes of faith and doubt centered on the Creation Museum and a re-creation of Noah's Ark in Kentucky. Built by a parachurch organization called Answers in Genesis, a group with belief in Young Earth creationism, these two parks are adamant assertions that if you do not believe in a fundamentalist interpretation of Genesis and the Bible, you will not be saved. The Creation Museum's visualization of this belief in the literal timeline of Genesis results in life-size wax figures of humans existing alongside dinosaurs, and at the Ark Encounter the single, dominating door in the facade of the Noah's Ark re-creation signals the one way into salvation. Such visualizations, along with Answers in Genesis's public campaign against mainstream or consensus science, become grounds for counter and doubt. *MAD* magazine's parody cartoon "Charles Darwin's Night at the Creation Museum" co-opts the imagery of the *Night at the Museum* movie poster to depict Charles Darwin's imagined horror at what the Creation Museum and Answers in Genesis espouse. Here, the parody treads on humor but also blasphemy. Whereas "Touchdown Jesus" might inspire self-reflection from insider Catholics and whereas the LDS Church might engage with its critics, Answers in Genesis and those who react against their beliefs yield no compromise. These landscapes of faith and doubt are absolutist in their messages. They demand of us to choose what we believe about the origin of the world and the nature of creation.

Finally, we see how a landscape of faith can be used to hide beliefs that are inimical to the very faith it promotes. Visitors to the giant, 65.5-foot *Christ of the Ozarks* statue in Eureka Springs, Arkansas, most often see the statue as an homage and celebration of Jesus Christ, whose supersized, outstretched arms visualize Jesus's benediction of the United States. Many visitors approach this statue as a sacred object and with reverence, while others snicker at its awkward proportions and inartful sculpture, generating the nicknames "Milk Carton Jesus" and "Gumby Jesus," a reference to the green clay animation figure pervasive in American popular culture. Yet most visitors do not know the anti-Semitic, racist, hate-filled beliefs of the statue's creator, Gerald L. K. Smith, whose grave near the statue all visitors pass by. The nicknames "Milk Carton Jesus" and "Gumby Jesus" further shift the focus from Smith's beliefs to a narrow aesthetic judgment of the statue. Smith created a larger evangelical theme park on the Arkansas mountaintop with a popular Passion play performed on an elaborate stage set of Old Jerusalem with 150 actors and live animals; a New Holy Land tour through re-creations of the Middle East of Jesus's time; a "Christ Only Art Gallery"; and a Bible Museum. While a celebration of Christ and Christianity, Smith's "sacred projects" nevertheless foregrounded his anti-Semitic views, including intimation in the Passion play blaming Jews for the death of Jesus. Smith claimed that the *Christ of the Ozarks* statue had been the subject of bomb threats, which while never carried out were a powerful, imagined visual response of erasure and censure to a landscape of faith. The complex landscapes of faith and doubt, of right and wrong belief, and our unwitting complicity in our consumption of the beliefs the *Christ of the Ozarks* statue embodied is the subject of chapter 5.

This book's approach focuses on the personal, asking how we encounter, question, and react to religion in our daily lives. It does not take a larger frame of how these landscapes of faith and doubt may make claims on America's professed value of religious pluralism, and it does not consider the political dimensions of these reactions or the nature of the cultural wars they may represent.[28] Nor does this book delve deeply into the theory of religious satire and parody especially as applied to visual culture. This is not to say this work does not need to be done—it very much does with respect to these examples. What I offer here is a starting point of looking closely at the visual components of religious doubt.

The variety of landscapes of doubt in this book resonates with the "powerful yet diffuse imaginations" Dell Upton describes in cultural landscapes. Landscapes of doubt are born from many viewpoints drawing on an array of popular culture and mass media references and on a spectrum from humor to blasphemy. We see insider and outsider audiences that intersect and overlap. We see generators of doubt who are professionalized with mass media platforms—cartoons, publications, television shows—and other generators who are anonymous with more local reaches. We see what can be humorous to one audience can be profoundly hurtful to another, and that some landscapes of doubt engage while others simply attack. The power of landscapes of doubt is that they make the questions about religion and belief immediate and visible to us, engaging us in a conversation about the transcendent and the immanent. The 900-foot Jesus—along with "Touchdown Jesus," *The Wizard of Oz* Mormon temple, Jerry Falwell's waterslide plunge photograph, *The Simpson*'s "Praiseland" episode, *Doonesbury*'s Oral Roberts "Death Watch" cartoon, "Charles Darwin's Night at the Creation Museum" parody image, and "Gumby Jesus"—activates our religious built environment in ways unanticipated but illuminating, asking us, at times forcefully, to consider and clarify what it is we believe.[29]

A final note: Some entities declined to grant permission to publish images in this book, specifically stills of Dorothy, the Yellow Brick Road, and the Wizard of Oz from the 1939 movie *The Wizard of Oz* (copyright owned by Warner Bros.); a still of the Praiseland theme park from the 2001 "I'm Goin' to Praiseland" episode of *The Simpsons* (copyright owned by Twentieth Century Fox Film Corporation); and the 2007 "Charles Darwin's Night at the Creation Museum" cartoon in *MAD* magazine (copyright owned by DC Entertainment). Reasons for these refusals remain unclear, and such refusals speak to the difficulty for scholars writing on the visual components of popular culture and sensitive issues surrounding religion. I am hopeful readers will seek out these images readily available online and in other sources to better understand the analysis of them offered here.

# 1

# TOUCHDOWN JESUS!

For the nearly 80,000 football fans in the University of Notre Dame stadium and three million more watching on national television on a picturesque fall Saturday in 2014, the view toward the northern end zone offered a spectacular vision (fig. 2). Just beyond the stadium boundary, Jesus Christ rose above the scoreboard, his arms outstretched as if ordaining Notre Dame's football triumph. This view of Jesus on a 132-foot mosaic mural, installed in 1964 and seen by millions since, has inspired the playfully irreverent nickname "Touchdown Jesus" that wittily intertwines Notre Dame's two defining traditions: football and Catholicism.

"Touchdown Jesus" is the enduring name for an altarpiece of an American sports culture that traffics in religious imagery and ritual. To experience a Notre Dame football game is to make a pilgrimage to the stadium, attend a pregame mass, engage in tailgating fellowship, cheer with religious fervor, and pray for the success of a Hail Mary pass. In *Touchdown Jesus: Faith and Fandom at Notre Dame,* Scott Eden plays on this metaphor of football as religion with the chapter titles "A Busload of Pilgrims," "The Liturgy and Devotions," "Messiahs and Pariahs," and "The Wailing Wall."[1] R. Laurence Moore's *Touchdown Jesus: The Mixing of Sacred and Secular in American History* similarly uses the mural as cover image and springboard to argue

"how easily religious Americans can entwine the sacred and the secular."[2] In sanctifying football, "Touchdown Jesus" captures the very real co-opting of religion in
American life.

While "Touchdown Jesus" has become the famous and even beloved moniker
for this mural, it is not the original name or intention for it.[3] The original intention
of the mural, formally entitled *The Word of Life,* on the facade of Notre Dame's
Memorial Library had little to do with football. Together, the mural and skyscraper library set out to position the University of Notre Dame as a great modern
American university in academic, not athletic, reputation in the modernizing era
of the Second Vatican Council. The library's modern architecture and enormous
skyscraper tower were to signal the university as a major research institution. The
library's figurative mural showcased a large-scale image of a risen Christ to pro-
claim him as "The Word of Life," a reference to the opening lines of the Gospel of

John, and position the figure of Christ above a gathering of the major philosophers and theologians of every age, signaling Christ as the ultimate truth (fig. 3). Father Theodore Hesburgh and his administration believed that the library and mural communicated that it was possible for a university to be modern *and* religious, an idea already largely abandoned by American research universities in the mid-twentieth century for which scientific and empirical inquiry could not be sustained within a specifically Christian outlook.[4] For Father Hesburgh and his circle, the library and mural proclaimed that Notre Dame could be a great American university without leaving its Catholicism behind. But this was not necessarily the message the public understood in 1964, nor the message the American public intuits today.

The genesis of "Touchdown Jesus" highlights the unintended reception of religious images and architecture and the transformation in their meaning. For Father Theodore M. Hesburgh (1917–2015), under whose university presidency the library was constructed and after whom the library would be renamed in 1987, "Thinking of this as 'Touchdown Jesus' was just not in my mind or anybody else's for that matter."[5] Even if one suspects the positioning of the mural across from the stadium to be a brilliant publicity and proselytizing ploy, the "Touchdown Jesus" nomenclature apparently evolved from an accident in sight lines. The nickname arose out of the vernacular, with some accounts placing it in use among students shortly after the mural's unveiling in 1964. The nickname appeared in a University of Notre Dame student publication in 1968 and in a national

**Figure 3.** *The Word of Life* mural (1964) by artist Millard Sheets on the Theodore M. Hesburgh Library (1961–63), architects Ellerbe and Company, University of Notre Dame, Notre Dame, Indiana. (Photograph by Margaret M. Grubiak)

*Washington Post* sports story in 1969.[6] "Touchdown Jesus" demonstrates the power of audiences to remake and recast religious meaning.

What "Touchdown Jesus" means differs across audiences. Many people, including many Catholics, see the humor and wit in the "Touchdown Jesus" nickname and perceive it as a harmless description of Catholic sports culture. For others, "Touchdown Jesus" more seriously and authentically speaks to how sports mirror religion as a way to orient ourselves to the world. For still others, "Touchdown Jesus" operates as an idol to a false god, promoting prayer for false ends, and aligning Catholic values to a corrupt sports culture. In ways different and even more accessible than its official title *The Word of Life,* "Touchdown Jesus" brings to bear questions about the uses of religion and even what religion is.

### "Touchdown Jesus" and the Religion of Sports

"Touchdown Jesus" is a striking visible manifestation of how we imbue sports with religious language, space, and ritual. Consider sports teams' names that evoke gods, demons, and the supernatural: the Tennessee Titans, the Anaheim Angels, the Duke Blue Devils, the New Orleans Saints, the Washington Wizards. At Oral Roberts University in Tulsa, Oklahoma, the basketball stadium includes a direct expression of faith with the phrase "Expect a Miracle" emblazoned on the baseline of its basketball stadium, a reminder of a core belief of Oral Roberts and Pentecostalism.[7] In California, the Los Angeles Angels' religious identity is made visible in their stadium sign, whose supergraphic *A* is ringed by a halo (fig. 4). We can read the stadia of sports as religious temples, the pitcher's mound as a "comic mountain" in the Mircea Eliade sense of an organizing center from which an imagined cosmos is generated, and the four bases as the four corners of the world.[8] Super Bowl Sunday, the World Series, the NCAA Basketball Championship, and college football game day are rituals around which we center our national life.

These messy boundaries between sports and religion transform our conception about what religion can be. In *The Joy of Sports,* theologian Michael Novak calls sports "a form of religion" because they provide "organized institutions, disciplines, and liturgies" and attract followers who enact those rituals and become devoted to their teams.[9] Like religion, sports, as theologian Joseph Price observes, "estab-

lish means for bonding in communal relations with other devotees."[10] In this way, sports help form an American civil religion as Robert Bellah first outlined in the 1960s, uniting Americans in a religiously imbued nationalism carried out in the performance of the national anthem at the start of games and in shared national events such as Super Bowl Sunday. Sports also engage the theological structure of traditional religions. Games are a microcosm of life played out in two halves, four quarters, or seven innings. Michael Novak argues that sports "recreate symbols of cosmic struggle, in which human survival and moral courage are not assured" and, as Price suggests, "model ways to deal with contingencies and fate while playing by the rules."[11] Sports mirror the cycle of death, rebirth, and redemption inherent in religious sacraments such as the Eucharist and baptism "wherein the communicants

**Figure 4.** Anaheim Stadium, Anaheim, California, with a halo ringing the super-graphic *A* symbolizing the Los Angeles Angels. (Photograph by Cynthia Lujan published by Continental Postcard Co., postcard in the personal collection of Margaret M. Grubiak)

symbolically experience death and rebirth."[12] Defeat in sports, as Novak writes, "symbolizes death, and it certainly feels like dying," while victory in sports allows us to sample, in Price's view, "at least in an anticipatory way, 'abundant life'" promised in the afterlife.[13] Sports can instill values in the way that religion aims to do. Sports "teach religious qualities of heart and soul" and the formation of character in lessons of bravery, courage, survival, perseverance, defeat, and grace.[14] As Price observes, sports "enable participants to explore levels of selfhood that otherwise remain inaccessible."[15] Operating in their own sense of sacred time and with their own rituals, sports in this view craft a world of action and belief in a way that we can read as nearly indistinguishable from religion. In this sense, sport *is* religion.

Yet other scholars are careful to maintain sports and religion as having distinct identities. Jeffrey Scholes and Raphael Sassower see sports and religion within the same "cultural web" in a "postsecular, late capitalist world."[16] While Joseph Price notes that scholars have variously described sports as popular religion, folk religion, cultural religion, and civil religion—a suggestion that the underlying impetus of people's interest in sports is a religious one—for Scholes and Sassower "sports does not *replace* religion nor is it merely 'religion in disguise.'"[17] David Morgan broadens this idea by suggesting that what we typically think of as making sports *religious* is instead making sports *sacred* or *special,* which is not the same as religious. As Morgan claims, "sacralization is not synonymous with religion nor it is essentially religious, but is rather the pervasive social mechanism for making something, someone, or someplace special."[18] Scholes, Sassower, and Morgan create room to think about how sports and religion have distinct identities even as they operate in similar ways, in the same cultural web of meaning. And yet, "Touchdown Jesus"—an image and nickname that overtly marries Christ and football—challenges this distinction. What Scholes, Sassower, and Morgan foreground for us, however, is that "Touchdown Jesus" is very much a cultural construction generated by real people, whether Catholic insiders or outsiders.

"Touchdown Jesus" becomes a visible part of a landscape of faith within this comingling of religion and sports. First, "Touchdown Jesus" makes the supernatural visible and present on the grounds of the University of Notre Dame within its most prized event. In depicting the figure of Jesus, the mural asserts the historical and theological reality of Jesus in the world. A nearby plaque explaining the mural gives witness to the Incarnation through human senses: "Became man of the Blessed Virgin, He was seen and looked upon by human eyes and His voice was heard upon the earth" (see fig. 8).[19] The representation of Jesus in the mural recalls this reality of Christ—and, in the Catholic understanding of the Holy Trinity, by extension also God and the Holy Spirit—but also suggests his immanence in our present day, not just in historical time. As Jesus peeks over the football stadium's northern goalpost, his arms upraised in a perpetual motion of blessing, "it is understood by many that the giant mural of Jesus watches over the shoulder of the coaches, players, and officials, thus providing Notre Dame with a number of miraculous victories."[20] In the image of "Touchdown Jesus," Jesus is actively rooting for Notre Dame (and against its opponents) in a mirroring of the actions of the Notre Dame fans gathered in the shadow of the mural. "Touchdown Jesus" represents a view of religion, and of Christianity, where our concerns are God's concerns and our passions his too—even football.

Second, "Touchdown Jesus" is an invitation and aid to prayer in this football-centered landscape of belief. The Notre Dame faithful "have been known to implore the heavens for a victory for the Fighting Irish," reciting the "Our Father" and "Hail Mary" as an appeal for Jesus to intercede on the field.[21] Fans have bestowed another tongue-in-cheek nickname on the mural as the "the world's largest holy card," an object of material religion more commonly the size of a playing card with images of Jesus and the saints used to focus religious devotion and memorialize the deceased.[22] For Notre Dame's coaches and athletes particularly, the centrality of prayer and religious belief conveyed in the oversized holy card spurs the belief that they can accomplish the seemingly impossible on the field, paying dividends on game day. "Touchdown Jesus" is an aid to prayer; a motivator of the highest order; a talisman for good fortune; and the ultimate trump card against opponents on the field of home court advantage.

Finally, "Touchdown Jesus" is also the organizing object of ritual for the University of Notre Dame's football and its Catholicism. On home game days, the players and coaches march from their training complex, past Hesburgh Library and the "Touchdown Jesus" mural, and to the northern gates of the stadium in a ritual known as the "Player Walk." Fans and well-wishers line the procession, offering benedictions to the players via high-fives as bagpipes fill the air with solemnity. Heightening the religious aspect of this ritual, the quadrangle between the library and the stadium forms an outdoor church with the mural as the focal point. The events hosted in the quadrangle are evidence of its understanding as a religious space broadly construed: the quadrangle has served as the setting for a pontifical mass celebrating the library's opening in 1964 and the 9/11 Memorial Mass in 2011, and it also has hosted Friday football pep rallies and ESPN's College GameDay.[23]

In these three functions—making the supernatural present, aiding prayer, and organizing ritual—"Touchdown Jesus" is a centerpiece of a landscape of faith centered on the religion of sports. For the Notre Dame faithful who revel in the culture of football and religion, "Touchdown Jesus" is an affirmation and continuation of Catholic belief applied to sports. For many, "Touchdown Jesus" is an accurate naming of how religion works in their lives.

## "Touchdown Jesus" in the Landscape of Doubt

The generally positive reception and continued replication of the "Touchdown Jesus" name in this landscape of a sports faith overshadows another, more doubtful reception of the mural that raises significant questions about the nature of religion. When we understand the nickname "Touchdown Jesus" from the posture of doubt, the mural challenges us to think through questions of how we valorize sports at the expense of other concerns; how we use prayer and to what end; how Catholics in particular use religious images; and how the values of sports misalign with the values of religion. Rather than merely witty or humorous, the very imagery of "Touchdown Jesus" can be read as idolatrous and emblematic of a false religion. In these readings of "Touchdown Jesus" from the perspective of doubt and questioning, the renamed mural does not appear merely humorous or witty, but rather revealing of weighty concerns and criticism over how religion should operate versus how it actually does.

The name "Touchdown Jesus" suggests that Jesus's attention is devoted to trivial concerns over more important issues in the world—a critique has been the topic of sports reporting. In 1990, the Fighting Irish won games against rivals Michigan and Michigan State with seemingly miraculous last-minute saves amid what a *Chicago*

*Tribune* reporter called a "chorus of 'Hail Marys'" and "many prayers to 'Touchdown Jesus.'"[24] The reporter sought out theologians to address the question "Is the Blessed Mother calling plays for the Irish?" Protestant theologian and University of Chicago religious historian Martin Marty answered no to the question, arguing that we cannot expect to direct God's attention to a specific event or cause: "We can never be specific as to say that God's care is applied to a specific event—even those events that are as serious, especially in some people's minds, as Notre Dame football."[25] To further this point about directing prayer to a particular outcome, the theologians interviewed in the *Chicago Tribune* story posited that if we see Notre Dame's victories as a sign of God's attention, then we must also see Notre Dame's losses as a lack of God's attention.[26] A 1998 *Sports Illustrated* article posed a similar question—"Does God Care Who Wins the Super Bowl?"—to which Vanderbilt Divinity School dean Joseph C. Hough firmly answered no with a sharp rebuke: "I don't think God intervenes to make anybody win over anybody else, just like I don't think God makes people win wars over anybody else. This kind of ritual enactment to manipulate God is really anti-Christian at its core."[27] Yale Divinity School dean Richard J. Wood leveled an even more scathing assessment of the idea that God cares about sports in the context of late 1990s world events: "We have a terrible war going on in Bosnia and the persecution of Christians in Indonesia and the genocide in Rwanda, and to suggest, in that light, that God has a direct involvement in athletic contests trivializes the whole notion of God's involvement with the world. It is a heresy."[28] In this view, "Touchdown Jesus" is foolish, even heretical, for its suggestion that God is concerned about the outcome of a mere football game.

The very insertion of prayer in sports suggested by "Touchdown Jesus" and "Hail Mary" passes calls into question the proper uses of religion and faith. For the Catholic Reverend Richard P. McBrien, chair of the theology department at Notre Dame in 1990, praying to Jesus and the Blessed Virgin Mary at football games was "all part of the Notre Dame myth" and was fine "as long as these things aren't taken seriously." It is when we take prayers directing God to intervene in sport seriously that "you're on dangerous ground."[29] While some offer prayers in sporting events to realize players' best abilities, ensure the safety of all players on the field, or simply express joy—prayers that on the face of it seem proper and in order—others pray to ask for the victory of a particular team, suggesting that God is actively rooting against the other team in a zero-sum game. This prayer for one's own victory is a perversion of prayer for selfish ends. As Shirl Hoffman argues, "Some athletic prayers seem inauthentic because they are so crassly opportunistic."[30] And to some, the public display of prayer in sports, as in a player taking a knee in prayer in the end zone, is not proper prayer because it is the opposite of humility before God.[31] Finally, prayer in sports can also veer from asking for the intercession of God to mere superstition, as in the rituals some players undertake to ward off bad luck. "Touchdown Jesus" suggests that we can manipulate God's will and misuse prayer through selfishness, pride, or superstition.

"Touchdown Jesus" also aligns Catholicism and Christianity generally with antithetical and corruptive values embodied in modern collegiate sports. Before widely embracing sports in the twentieth century, American religious leaders believed sports were in conflict with religion: they promoted brutality and gambling; they occupied energy and focus that might otherwise be applied to the creation of moral character and service to and study of God; and they threatened church attendance on Sundays.[32] In the twentieth century, some religious groups came to see sports as ways to develop moral character, as in the "muscular Christianity" and "sportaneity" movements and the Fellowship of Christian Athletes, founded in 1954.[33] Within Catholic circles, Popes John Paul II and Benedict XVI wrote about the joys and benefits of engaging in sports, and the Pontifical Council of the Laity's section on "Church and Sport," instituted in 2004, also sees sports as a means for unity, peace, and Christian witness.[34] Julie Bryne's account of three national championships of the Catholic Immaculata College women's basketball team in the 1970s suggests the ways that faith, sport, and education can go hand-in-hand.[35] At Princeton University, the 1913 statue by sculptor Daniel Chester French nicknamed "The Christian Student" celebrated hero Princetonian W. Earl Dodge for being both the captain of the championship Princeton football team and the leading founder of the Intercollegiate Young Men's Christian Association.[36] The "Christian Student" valorized the combination of intellectual achievement, athletic skill, and spirituality in an ideal young man. But modern-day sports has transformed play into big-time sports in universities, whose primary focus is not on the moral development of athletes but rather the enormous budgets for coaches' salaries, state-of-the-art athletic complexes, massive television contracts, and the eclipsing of academics as the very reason for the existence of the university.[37] (To this point, "The Christian Student," now located in the lobby of Princeton's Jadwin Gymnasium, has been renamed "The Princeton Student" in an overshadowing of its Christian identity.) In 2009, the University of Notre Dame ranked 27th out of the top 100 American universities with the largest expenditures on athletic programs, with Notre Dame spending $64.7 million in that year.[38] These immense athletic budgets, along with the great publicity that university sports teams generate and capture, shift the focus toward entertainment or even profit as the university's raison d'être.[39] For Robert Higgs, the culture of modern-day, big-time collegiate football at Notre Dame is at odds with its Catholic values: the University of Notre Dame's "seduction by bowl committees betrays a lust for worldly power, praise, and money that Thomas More repeatedly indicted."[40] For Jesus—the embodiment of humility, power in the next world rather than this one, and spiritual wealth and material poverty—to be connected with big-time sports is the highest irony of "Touchdown Jesus."

By suggesting a god devoted to football rather than Christianity, "Touchdown Jesus" appears nakedly idolatrous. Jesus's upturned arms position him as a referee in judgment of a mere game, as a god of football. The mural in this view is evidence of a "false religion," a violation of the first commandment of having no other gods beside the one and only God. Although theologians Michael Novak, Joseph Price, and others have theorized sports as a religion unto themselves—for the ways, as we have seen, sports mirror the institutional structures of religion, mimic grand schemes of life and death, and allow players and fans alike to experience other dimensions of the self—an alternative understanding is that the very idea of sports as a religion is blasphemous. Those who do not subscribe to the idea of sports as a religion counter that sports cannot be a religion because there is no agreed upon understanding of a higher purpose, no transformational aspect of sports beyond this earthy realm, and no sacramental function.[41] In this view "Touchdown Jesus" is a false idol of the false religion of sports.

And for some Protestants who see the image, "Touchdown Jesus" can be viewed as idolatrous for its very imaging of Christ, a violation of the commandment against "graven images" central to Reformed Protestant belief. The sixteenth-century Protestant Reformation targeted images of Jesus and Mary, the so-called cult of the saints, and the nature of the Catholic mass as a way to correct the perceived corruptions of Catholic piety. More broadly, as historian Carlos Eire has argued, the Reformation represented a shift from Catholicism's "religion of immanence" to Protestantism's "religion of transcendence" that had profound consequences for the relationship between the material and the spiritual.[42] For Catholics, images of Christ, Mary, and the saints materially realized Catholic belief of God's presence in the world, with intercession available at every point and heaven "never too far from earth."[43] The Reformed Protestantism of John Calvin and Ulrich Zwingli believed solely in a religion of transcendence in which "the finite cannot contain the infinite," placing the emphasis on word rather than visual object.[44] But the Protestant relationship with images is more complicated, as scholars of material religion have shown, and Protestantism is not aniconic, as is often assumed. An important Protestant visual culture existed from the Reformation forward that replaced, for example, images of Christ with images of Martin Luther and promoted mass-produced religious images though consciously combined with text.[45] As John Davis has explored, nineteenth-century American Protestants experiencing "Catholic envy" viewed Catholic art, churches, and ritual at home or while traveling to Rome "to sample and to taste" the "exotic" religious other but "with the expectation that there would be a retreat back to the familiar world of Protestant boundaries, a world embraced its rationality and decorum."[46] In the twentieth century, Protestants and others consumed artist Warner Sallman's famed *Head of Christ* painting at the scale of 500 million reproductions by the mid-1980s.[47] As we see in chapter 5, the 1966 *Christ of the Ozarks* statue that dominates the hills of Eureka Springs, Arkansas, was at the behest of Gerald L. K. Smith, an ordained minister in the Disciples of Christ of the Reformed Protestant tradition (see fig. 46). Smith rationalized that his statue would not "encourage imagery" and assured that while "this image is not our Lord," "every time we look upon it it reminds us of His deity, His grace, His love and His saving power."[48] These examples show that Protestants across traditions, whether Lutheran or Reformed, produced and consumed images of Christ in both domestic and public spheres. But "Touchdown Jesus" in its public, Catholic context raised the specter of Catholic idolatry at root in Protestant identity, irrespective of how Protestants themselves used images. "Touchdown Jesus" from this perspective figures Christ in a form of devotion judged as wrong.

While many may understand *The Word of Life* mural as "Touchdown Jesus" and simply smile at its humor and move on, for others the nickname as well as the image itself give us pause to question how we use religion. In this landscape of doubt, "Touchdown Jesus" asks us to think about how we use and misuse prayer; what kinds of values sports uphold, and if Christianity should endorse them; and how we may create false gods to a false religion. Like other landscapes of faith and doubt, "Touchdown Jesus" asks us to confront and judge right and wrong belief.

## The Original Intention of "Touchdown Jesus"

"Touchdown Jesus" worked against the mural's intended purpose to correct the perception and stereotypes of Catholics' diminished role in American intellectual life in the mid-twentieth century. Historian Richard Hofstadter wrote bitingly in *Anti-Intellectualism in American Life,* published in 1963, one year before the Notre Dame mural's unveiling, about American Catholicism's "cultural impoverishment, its non-intellectualism" and asserted that "the intellectual achievement of Catholic colleges and universities remains startlingly low."[49] Hofstadter reported that Catholic educators and supporters "have been dismayed to see Catholic schools commonly reproducing the vocationalism, athleticism, and anti-intellectualism which prevails so widely in American higher education as a whole."[50] Hofstadter cited his source as a 1955 article by Catholic monsignor John Tracy Ellis, who claimed "the failure of American Catholics to make a notable mark upon the intellectual life of their country."[51]

Such a perception of anti-intellectualism in American Catholic culture was precisely what *The Word of Life* mural was to counter before its reframing as "Touchdown Jesus." *The Word of Life* mural was of a piece with the Second Vatican Council, which over a series of meetings from 1962 to 1965 called for a renewal of Catholicism and the Church's greater engagement in the contemporary world. From Vatican II came an acknowledgment of the importance of scholarship and learning produced in secular universities, thus validating Catholic institutions that sought to model their own achievement on the standards of secular universities, much as Notre Dame modeled itself on Princeton, and to counter the anti-intellectualism pointed out by Hofstadter.[52] Contrary to previous conceptions about the dangers of free and open inquiry to the Catholic faith, the Second Vatican Council supported academic freedom essential to the creation of a modern, Catholic university. This delicate balancing was particularly clear in Pope Paul VI's blessing for Notre Dame's library at its opening in 1964: "The quest for truth requires freedom; but it must be borne in mind that the freedom of a Catholic university in seeking and spreading truth must always respect the limits imposed by the law of charity, of justice, and of human dignity." While clearly stating the "sacred duty of Catholic professors and students to follow the Church's authentic magisterium in matters of faith and morals," Pope Paul VI carefully stressed that such obedience would not "prove to be a detriment to science or to freedom; rather will it be a safeguard for the supreme human and Christian values, and exalt the prestige of the Catholic university."[53] The new library—with its modern architecture and Christocentric mural—spoke explicitly to the balance between modernization and keeping God central in academic inquiry that the modern Notre Dame and Father Hesburgh sought.

Raising the University of Notre Dame's academic reputation above its athletic prowess was a central goal of Father Theodore Hesburgh's thirty-five-year presidency from 1952 to 1987. When Hesburgh first took office, the shadow of Notre Dame football loomed large. Driven by the success of such legendary figures as Knute Rockne, football had become a critically important publicity, fundraising, and recruiting tool for Notre Dame. Football captured the public's attention, reinforced the loyalty (and contributions) of alumni, and attracted the most talented of the nation's Catholic students to the university. These benefits of a strong athletic program notwithstanding, Hesburgh wished to recast Notre Dame's postwar identity as a thriving research institution ranking among the best American universities. Constructing a large, modern library plainly signaled this ambition. Despite Father Hesburgh's denial that the view of the library and its mural from the stadium was intentional, observers recognized early on that the library "symbolically competes with the football stadium for the dominant image of the campus."[54] The library and stadium visualized the competing claims to the university's identity.

As president during the unsettled era of the Vietnam War and student protests, Hesburgh straddled a fine line between progress and maintaining the university's Catholic identity. The title of a 1969 *New York Times Sunday Magazine* article on the president highlighted the contrasting views on President Hesburgh: "Hesburgh of Notre Dame—(1) 'He's Destroying This University' (2) 'He's Bringing It into the Mainstream of American Life.'" Published five years after the dedication of *The Word of Life* mural and the library, the article by Thomas Fleming cited Hesburgh's desire to transform "Notre Dame from a football factory to a first-rate university." Part of this transformation was letting go of strictures on student life. Hesburgh eliminated mass checks (proof that students had attended religious services), ended the lights-out policy, and allowed dorm room visits by the opposite sex.[55] In making these changes, Hesburgh followed the lead of other American universities, even if these changes came a few decades later and were less pronounced in this denominational school. Other significant changes would also occur in Hesburgh's term: the University of Notre Dame first admitted undergraduate women in 1972.

More importantly, Hesburgh helped raise the University of Notre Dame as an intellectual peer of other American universities, an equality that sometimes seemed at odds with the university's Catholic identity. As Fleming wrote, "Until Theodore Hesburgh arrived on the scene, Notre Dame and every other Catholic university were aliens in this [university] world because they did not subscribe to its basic tenet: relentless and even ruthless pursuit of the truth, no matter how hard or unpleasant the conclusions."[56] Prior to the mid-twentieth century, Catholic universities had sometimes disengaged from difficult questions or disallowed full and open intellectual inquiry when such inquiry challenged church teaching. "Faith," as Fleming summarized the Catholic position, "was too precious to risk exposing it to the 'godless' rationalism of American secular thought."[57] As we have seen in the voice of Richard Hofstadter, pervasive was the perception of Catholic education as intellectually weak.[58] Father Hesburgh emerged as a staunch voice for academic freedom in Catholic higher education.[59] Echoing the sentiments of Pope Paul VI, Hesburgh repeatedly affirmed that faculty and students within the university needed to be free to question everything: man could not fulfill his potential "unless he is free to follow any argument, any research, any point of inquiry, wherever it may lead."[60] But this freedom did not mean a loss of Catholic perspective. Rather, "We must somehow match secular or state universities in their comprehension of a vast spectrum of natural truths in the arts and sciences, while at the same time we must be in full possession of our own true heritage of theological wisdom."[61]

To build Notre Dame's academic program, the Hesburgh administration launched a series of bold fundraising campaigns beginning with the 1958 "Program for the Future." Also known as Challenge I, the "Program for the Future" aimed to raise $66.6 million over ten years.[62] The campaign's focus clearly showed the shift of priorities away from athletics. The "top priority projects" included funding for two graduate residence halls, student aid, and faculty and administration development, but the campaign's highest priority was the new library. A $6 million award from the Ford Foundation in 1960 accelerated the campaign's momentum and the library's construction schedule. The Ford Foundation selected the University of Notre Dame as an institution whose leadership and development programs were "commensurate in scope, imagination, and practicability to the vast need of American society." The grant put Notre Dame in the company of other major private American universities including Stanford University and Johns Hopkins University, which also received Ford Foundation grants.[63] This recognition signaled Notre Dame's emerging promise on the national stage. Saying the support enabled Notre Dame "to take a great leap forward in its striving for academic excellence," Hesburgh expressed gratitude to the Ford Foundation in helping Notre Dame and others "to be beacons of intellectual achievement, to raise up competent scholars, scientists, professional men, teachers, leaders in public and industrial life, to set the sure pattern of morally responsible and capable person emerging from among the greatest resource of America: our young people."[64] Hesburgh here carefully set out Notre Dame's mission in terms conspicuously distinct from game day results. In Hesburgh's view, the University of Notre Dame was called to shape national life in the second half of the twentieth century.

The proposed new library symbolized the progressive, modern, and influential Notre Dame at midcentury. Designed to serve both undergraduate and graduate students as well as support faculty research, the library would replace Lemonnier Library, a 1917 neo-classical structure overwhelmed by the needs of a university five times the size by the 1960s. Father Hesburgh made clear that the old library no longer supported Notre Dame's academic mission, calling it "completely out-of-date for today's Notre Dame."[65] The proposed skyscraper library put forward a self-consciously modern image (fig. 5). It was to be the "largest and tallest" building on the Notre Dame campus at thirteen stories, nearly matching the height of the golden dome atop the Main Building, the symbol of Notre Dame and source of the "Domer" nickname for Notre Dame students. The library was "the next step in

the steady march toward ever-higher academic achievement" and essential to this aim since, in the familiar adage of many a university president and head librarian, "it is difficult to conceive of a truly great university without a correspondingly great library."[66]

The choice of modernism for the library's style was a purposeful articulation of Notre Dame's "Program for the Future." The design for the new library by Minnesota architectural firm Ellerbe and Company fulfilled head librarian Victor Schaefer's mandate that "the library must be functional for 'form follows function.'"[67] In citing Chicago architect Louis Sullivan's famed maxim, Schaefer voiced what had become a mantra for twentieth-century modernism. Schaefer wanted the building to work, and to work well, as a modern library. Ellerbe and Company delivered a building whose two-part organization, in true modernist fashion, "discloses the functional organization of the library's services within."[68] The architects created an eleven-story tower for the Research Library, housing more specialized resources for graduate students and faculty including semi-closed stacks, study carrels, seminar rooms, specialized libraries, and faculty offices. The U-shaped, two-story base, each story one acre, catered to undergraduates, housing open stacks, study rooms, an Audio Learning Center, and resources of the College Library. The references made to masters of modernism in the library are many: the use of lavish stone recalls Ludwig Mies van der Rohe; the tower atop a plinth, the organization of the Lever House by Gordon Bunshaft of Skidmore, Owings and Merrill; the use of pilotis and the harshness of its massing, both early and late Le Corbusier. Ellerbe and Company clearly asserted a modernist lineage for the library, adapting modern corporate land-marks to academic purposes, transferring their modernity to Notre Dame itself, and casting the library as bearer of the most current academic resources available. Given the building's immense size, there was no question as to the number of resources the university devoted to this central symbol of knowledge. In architectural image and size, the library announced its modernity and proclaimed it as central in the skyline of the university.[69]

## The Genesis of *The Word of Life*

For Father Theodore Hesburgh and university administrators, the library's mod-ernist architectural form alone did not sufficiently communicate the whole of the library's intention to raise Notre Dame's academic and intellectual standing. The library's harsh architecture and enormous vertical presence and size spawned the monikers "brain silo," "Mount Excellence," and, in a nod to Father Hesburgh's key role in the library's creation, "Ted's Mahal." But perhaps the most worrisome nick-name was "the largest grain elevator in the Midwest."[70] Father Hesburgh and the architects were concerned with creating a visual identity for the skyscraper library in the midwestern landscape beyond its modernist and even utilitarian-appearing image. Hesburgh said practically, "We knew that if we didn't do something with this building that the enormity of it . . . the size could be mistaken for a grain elevator or something, especially out here."[71] For these reasons, a large-scale mosaic mural by artist Millard Sheets depicting Notre Dame's Catholic intellectual heritage—

realized at 132 feet tall and 68 feet wide and crafted from an impressive 6,000 to 7,000 granite pieces—was made part of the library's early conception.

In addition to this rather pragmatic rationale for the mural, *The Word of Life* mural had another very specific if surprising source—the mosaic murals of the Central Library at the Universidad Nacional Autónoma de México (UNAM) in Mexico City—that proved both a model and a polemical interlocutor for Father Hesburgh (fig. 6). Hesburgh, a self-professed "great visitor of universities worldwide," toured the UNAM campus in April 1955 where he was "struck by the façade" of the Mexican library.[72] The Central Library, designed by noted architect and artist Juan O'Gorman in collaboration with Gustavo Saavedra and Juan Martinez de Velasco, had been completed two years earlier in 1953. Like Ellerbe and Company's design for the Notre Dame library nearly a decade later, the Central Library also used a two-story base on top of which arose a ten-story, nearly windowless block for the book stacks. O'Gorman's colorful, figurative murals covering the library's tower enlivened

**Figure 6.** Mural by Juan O'Gorman on the southern facade of the Central Library (1951–53), Universidad Nacional Autónoma de México, Mexico City, Mexico. (David R. Frazier Photolibrary, Inc./ Alamy Stock Photo)

and relieved the monotony of the International Style book stack tower, offering a solution to Notre Dame's need to give its library an identity distinct from a grain elevator.

Yet Father Hesburgh's motivation to co-opt UNAM's murals ran deeper than a mere solution of how to make his library more visually interesting: Hesburgh wanted to create a large-scale mural on his library, one unquestionably Christian in focus, to counter the paganistic message he believed the UNAM murals conveyed. In 1964, Howard V. Phalin, *The Word of Life* mural donor, confirmed that Father Hesburgh "made mention of the paganistic outlook of the mural at the University of Mexico and thought there should be something in the United States to counter-act this."[73] Hesburgh himself stated his belief that the Mexican murals were "pagan in representation" and that there needed to be "something with Christian represen-tation."[74] Hesburgh's desire to assert an overt Christian, Catholic image in the uni-versity setting was a direct counter to the kind of university UNAM was. Whereas UNAM was founded in 1910 as a public university separate from the control of the Catholic Church in order to allow greater academic freedom, Hesburgh wanted his library and mural at the University of Notre Dame to show that academic freedom and Catholicism could indeed coexist and thrive together, and that Catholicism still had high relevance in modern intellectual life. *The Word of Life* mural, as an explicit contrast to the UNAM murals, reaffirmed the very idea of the Catholic university. It was also an explicit visualization of Catholic theology and a witness to Catholic truth that countered any secular or paganistic worldview, as a nearby plaque articu-lated: "From the symbol of all Christianity, the cross, emerges the figure of Christ, the greatest of teachers. He, the Word of Life, the only begotten of the Father was from the beginning, with Father and Holy Spirit, in eternal divine life. . . . Loving ears listened to His words, and minds were inspired to remember and to note them down, and the ineffable New Testament took shape: the deeds and words of Christ, the primary document of Christian wisdom, the World of Life, and life giving truth" (see fig. 8).

Hesburgh's suggestion that the Mexican murals had a "paganistic outlook" was rooted in the cultural, political, and religious views that the Universidad Nacio-nal Autónoma de México campus and the library murals embodied. The Ciudad Universitaria, or University City, constructed from 1950 to 1953, was "a showpiece of the Mexican government's achievements in modernizing the country" since the Mexican Revolution in 1910.[75] The campus strove to portray Mexican modernization while attempting to reinforce Mexican nationalism, resulting in campus that was, as a 1953 *Time* magazine article described it, "as modern as next year's car and as variegated as a Mexican market scene."[76] The prevailing use of International Style architecture—which privileges the universal over the local—peppered with mosaics from Mexican craft tradition expressed post-revolutionary Mexico's many contradictions, especially its desire to uphold its future alongside its past.[77] The UNAM library's murals read as a graphic retelling of Mexican history on the book stack tower, but Juan O'Gorman's history privileges the pre-Hispanic past over its Catholic identity. The vast expanses of the northern and southern walls, respectively, treat Mexico's pre-Hispanic era and its colonial era, representing the Aztec gods Tlaloc, Quetzalcoatl, Coatlicue, and Huitzilopochtli; the conquering Spanish in 1521; and the downfall of the Aztec civilization, symbolized by the eagle figure of Aztec emperor Cuauhtémoc plummeting to the bottom of the southern facade. The library block's shorter ends round out the narrative with the modern age. The western end proclaims the UNAM crest as the symbol of the future of education, while the eastern end features a dove above a splitting atom and images of the Mexican revolution with the proclamations "Long Live the Revolution" and "Land and Liberty." Significantly, on this eastern end, O'Gorman featured the rising eagle figure of Cuauhtémoc "to say that Mexico is a country that was colonial, but that now it is not in the modern age."[78] For O'Gorman, Mexican independence and modernity meant a reassertion of Mexico's Mesoamerican, pre-Hispanic, pre-Christian past.[79]

The UNAM library's well-known mural on its southern elevation most likely provoked Hesburgh's "paganistic" judgment (see fig. 6). For this facade narrative of Mexico's colonial era, O'Gorman asked himself, "What did the Spanish bring to Mexico? They brought the cross and the Christianity based on the principle of the good and the bad."[80] To express the good and the bad, O'Gorman created two circles encompassing two differing cosmological views on man's position in the world: Ptolemy, who placed the Earth at the center of the universe, and Copernicus, for whom the sun was the center of the universe. O'Gorman equated Ptolemy with "the good, the faith" and Copernicus with "the bad, the science."[81] In casting the Spanish—and by extension Catholic—worldview as good versus bad and faith versus science on a university campus, O'Gorman portrayed an inimical relationship between Catholicism and academic inquiry, which was exactly the kind of relationship the University of Notre Dame wished to counter. Also significant is O'Gorman's visualization of religion itself. At the center of the southern facade is a temple on top of an Aztec pyramid "on whose base is instituted the Catholic Church."[82] To show Catholicism's origins within the Aztec religion, O'Gorman superimposed an image of a Catholic church with two towers onto the pyramid. The fact that a Catholic church is located at the bottom of the composition, surmounted by the pyramid and temple, and originates at the base of the pyramid suggests the enduring power of the pre-Christian religion in Mexican history.

Such a message is encoded at a larger scale. From afar, the southern facade becomes an abstract mask of the Aztec god Tlaloc. The giant circles describing O'Gorman's conception of the Catholic view on good and evil become Tlaloc's eyes, dominating the view from the main campus.[83] In recounting the history of the Spanish rule over Mexico, O'Gorman purposefully portrayed Mexican identity with a symbol from its polytheistic, and in Hesburg's view "paganistic," past.

In every way, *The Word of Life* mural by California artist Millard Sheets was a rebuke of and answer to UNAM's library murals. Christian images— a cross, the Christ figure, and light— give literal and symbolic organization to *The Word of Life* (fig. 7). Sheets, who had previously completed a mosaic mural for another Ellerbe and Company architectural commission, was sensitive to the need to provide an "architectonic" tie between the mural and the tower. His solution was to depict a cross, whose outline extends to the mural's edges, in the same color as the library tower. Just as the Aztec mask on the Mexican library tower is revealed on distant view, the cross is more apparent from afar (see fig. 3). Sheets overlaid a second "unifying form" with the Christ figure, the largest in the mural, positioned on the cross and at the top of the composition. With outstretched arms, Christ's body repeats the cross form while gathering the remaining fifty figures in a hierarchical arrangement. Light provides a third organizing structure. The mural's primary light source originates above Christ's head and runs through his upraised arms. Rays of light, skewed at harsh angles, cut the composition in Cubist fashion, casting the figures erratically into light and shadow. As Sheets explained, the diagonals are "the thought of Christ shedding light" and give "a kind of mystery and excitement to the composition as a whole."[84] These references made explicit Notre Dame's Christian, Catholic outlook.

The fifty-one figures in *The Word of Life* mural portray a history of truth and knowledge in which Christ, and the Christianity he embodies, are the culmination. The mural reads from bottom to top as a coalescing of scholars under Christ to illustrate "the roots, the foundation, and the growth of the Church."[85] Sheets stressed groups over individual figures; Christ is the mural's only named figure (fig. 8). In the lowest register, Sheets identified the roots of the church with groups of figures, read from left to right, from the Old Testament, the "Eastern World," the Medieval era, and "ancient classical cultures." In the mural's middle register, Sheets emphasized modernizing thought with figures from the Renaissance era, the "age of science and exploration," and the Byzantine era. Surmounting all of these figures in the mural's uppermost register are those celebrating the founding of the Catholic Church. Two groups each of the apostles and Christians of the early church nestle under Christ's upraised arms. In depicting a "never-ending line of great scholars, thinkers, and teachers" leading up to the "great teacher," Sheets crafted a narrative that acknowledged pre-Christian scholarship and the "continuous process of one generation giving to the next" while affirming, without apology, that truth ultimately resides in Christ.[86] As the plaque near the mural made clear, "With [Christ] in spirit are gathered the saints, the scholars, the scribes, and the teachers stretching through time, who have dedicated themselves to the preservation of truth, the Word of Life,

**Figure 8.** Explanatory plaque of *The Word of Life* mural, ca. 1964. (GPHR 45/5013, University Archives, University of Notre Dame, Notre Dame, Indiana)

and the preparation of men's minds to receive that truth."[87] The mural articulated for the University of Notre Dame a mission statement for the modern Catholic university, sanctioning academic freedom with the awareness and belief that Christ is its center and ultimate aim.

The irony of the very intentional Christian identity in *The Word of Life* is that the mural's transformation to "Touchdown Jesus" in the public's imagination carries its own paganistic overtones, just like the Aztec mask on the Mexican library tower. As we have seen, "Touchdown Jesus," irrespective of its figuring of Christ, can also be read as an idol to sport. In this view, Notre Dame fans worship multiple gods: the God of monotheistic Christianity and the god of sport. Just like Juan O'Gorman's murals mixing and interweaving Christianity with a polytheistic heritage, "Touchdown Jesus" similarly conveys a more complex message about what and who Notre Dame fans worship on game day. "Touchdown Jesus" in this way is more powerful than *The Word of Life* in revealing how the public receives the religious messages set out by the University of Notre Dame, both intentionally and unintentionally. The emphasis on "Touchdown Jesus" by the public over *The Word of Life* intended by the university administration reveals more fully how we practice religion in ways outside the carefully prescribed strictures of church and, in this case, university authorities.

"Touchdown Jesus" was created by the public out of a confluence of image, architecture, and space in ways unforeseen, and unintended, by the University of Notre Dame. For the University of Notre Dame administration, the library's architects, and the mural's artist, the creation of *The Word of Life* mural and its library canvas was a serious endeavor rooted in raising the academic profile of the university while maintaining its Catholic identity and intended to counteract the emphasis on Notre Dame football. Father Hesburgh and others denied that they were aware of the visual connection between the library and the stadium (fig. 9). As Father Hesburgh plainly said, "I had no idea of [the mural's] juxtaposition with the sta-

**Figure 9.** Aerial view of the University of Notre Dame with the library and *The Word of Life* mural on axis with the football stadium, ca. 1964. (GNDL 06/23, University Archives, University of Notre Dame, Notre Dame, Indiana)

dium; it never crossed my mind."[88] The library's location near the football stadium was determined largely by preexisting buildings, and the library's architects did not stress the connection between the library and the stadium. Among the surviving presentation drawings of the library by Ellerbe and Company is one beautifully rendered watercolor that shows two men conversing in the modernist interior of the penthouse lounge with views toward Notre Dame's hallmark buildings: the Main Building and the Basilica of the Sacred Heart, not the football stadium (fig. 10). In a purposeful exclusion of the stadium, Father Hesburgh said the view of the Main Building, the church, and the library together "makes a wonderful kind of trilogy to locate the university in its right position."[89] Photographs taken at the library's dedication in 1964 similarly ignored the relationship between library and stadium. Millard Sheets also gave careful thought to guiding the reception of his mural that had nothing to do with football. He designed an explanatory diagram—a three-panel plaque commemorating the mural's donors with a diagram numbering the groups of figures, a legend for these groups, and a three-paragraph description—on

**Figure 10.** Watercolor rendering of the Memorial Library penthouse, with views toward the University of Notre Dame's Basilica of the Sacred Heart and the Main Building rather than the football stadium, by Ellerbe and Company, ca. 1960. (UNDD Box G, University Archives, University of Notre Dame, Notre Dame, Indiana)

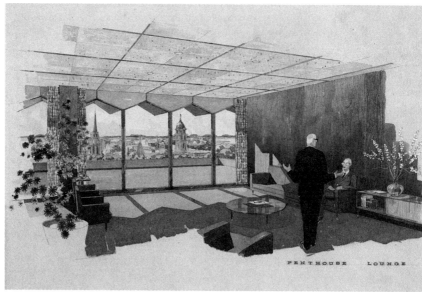

axis with the library's main entrance at the end of a shallow reflecting pool that places the viewer's back to the stadium, with football firmly out of view (see fig. 8). The experience of seeing *The Word of Life* was intended to be a contemplative one, not one amid the throngs of football fans.

But in the popular imagination, this was not what stuck. The much more accessible and immediately understandable "Touchdown Jesus" became the enduring name and frame through which the public viewed the mural. The weighty intentions of *The Word of Life* about raising the academic profile of Notre Dame, its engagement in the modernizing era of Vatican II, and its articulation of Catholic theology with Christ as the center of all truth was not what the public understood. Rather, "Touchdown Jesus" wittily blended Catholicism and football as Notre Dame's defining traditions. But the nickname carries its own weighty questions when viewed not simply as humorous but through the lens of doubt. "Touchdown Jesus" reveals deeper questions about sports as a religion; the specter of Catholic idolatry; the misuse of prayer; the values of sports versus the values of religion; and the status of Catholic intellectualism, one challenged by the overemphasis on sports.

# 2

## DOROTHY, *THE WIZARD OF OZ,* AND THE MORMON TEMPLE

Nearly every account of the enormous white building topped by six golden spires on Washington, D.C.'s Capital Beltway begins with a vivid description of how the building suddenly and majestically comes into view. Its siting takes full advantage of a rare straightaway on the outer loop of Interstate 495 in Maryland, so that the building, rising from the highway's horizon as drivers descend a hill, commands complete attention (fig. 11). Its gleaming marble exterior and dramatic lighting ensure its visibility at all hours. In a capital city crowded with monuments, this building finds a way to be singularly monumental to a captive audience of some 250,000 drivers daily, or nearly 60 million drivers a year.

For those who do not know it, coming upon this unexpected sight in the middle of negotiating the Capital Beltway can be perplexing. Other than a golden statue atop one of the spires whose identity is difficult to discern from a speeding car, the building has no obvious official signage to tell us what it is. In place of that, viewers are left to architecture by analogy—the association of a building with images well known in popular culture. To many, the building looks like a castle because of its abstracted crenellation (the signature up-and-down roofline of a castle) and because of its sharp, attenuated spires that appear lethal and defensive (fig. 12).[1] The lack of

visible exterior windows also emphasizes its fortress-like appearance, which earned the monikers "castle of refuge" and "mysterious citadel on the Beltway" in the press.[2] In the popular imagination, the building calls to mind Sleeping Beauty Castle at Disneyland and Cinderella Castle at Walt Disney World (fig. 13). The Disney comparison is not based on formal architectural similarities apart from the castellated form—the streamlined building on the D.C. Beltway certainly departs from the romantic, German-inspired Disney castles—but rather on the shared image of the fantastical and how these buildings engage our imaginations.

The building's other, more intriguing analogy made by the public is to the iconic 1939 movie *The Wizard of Oz* based on the book *The Wonderful Wizard of Oz,* the

**Figure 11.** View toward the Washington D.C. Temple of The Church of Jesus Christ of Latter-day Saints from the Interstate 495 Capital Beltway near Kensington, Maryland. (Kristina Blokhin/Alamy Stock Photo)

**Figure 12.** The Washington D.C. Temple of The Church of Jesus Christ of Latter-day Saints (1968–74), architects Fred L. Markham, Harold K. Beecher, Henry P. Fetzer, and Keith W. Wilcox, Kensington, Maryland. (Photograph by Margaret M. Grubiak)

first of fourteen Oz books author L. Frank Baum published between 1900 and 1920. While of course not the color green of the Emerald City depicted in the movie (one writer called the building "a bleached Emerald City of Oz"[3]) nor the Art Deco forms of the Royal Palace of Oz set, the building shares a strong sense of verticality and massing with the Oz palace in its multiple spires. We see the building within a forest from the highway, much as Dorothy sees the Emerald City within a field of poppies from the Yellow Brick Road (fig. 14).

If the visual analogy of the building to *The Wizard of Oz* was not enough, a nearby graffiti that reads "SURRENDER DOROTHY" makes the analogy explicit. This graffiti has a long, persistent history beginning in 1974, when before the building's dedication and during its public open house the phrase "SURRENDER DOROTHY" was spelled out in wadded-up newspaper on a highway bridge fence in sight of the building. This rogue act was reportedly the work of students from Holy

MONUMENTAL JESUS

**Figure 13.** Cinderella Castle (1970–71) in the Magic Kingdom, Walt Disney World, Orlando, Florida. (Zoonar GmbH/Alamy Stock Photo)

Child Catholic High School in nearby Potomac, Maryland, in a ploy to advertise their *Wizard of Oz* play.[4] Their temporary sign was then made permanent with painted letters on a railroad bridge over the Capital Beltway so that drivers see the words and the building simultaneously (fig. 15). This graffiti has been removed and repainted multiple times for more than four decades, demonstrating its continued resonance, and now includes the one-word stencil "SURRENDER."[5] It is a nod to a moment in *The Wizard of Oz* movie (which does not appear in the book) when the Wicked Witch of the West writes "SURRENDER DOROTHY" in the sky as Dorothy, Toto, the Tin Man, the Scarecrow, and the Lion look up from the Emerald City.[6]

MONUMENTAL JESUS

The Witch wanted Dorothy, whose falling house had killed the Witch's sister, the Wicked Witch of the East, when it landed in Oz, because Dorothy possessed the powerful, magical ruby red slippers—something the Wicked Witch of the West very much desired. Since Dorothy was in the Emerald City when the witch wrote the message, the "SURRENDER DOROTHY" graffiti identifies the building as the Palace of Oz within the Emerald City.

The implications of the building's analogy to *The Wizard of Oz* are profound when we realize this building is, in fact, the temple of The Church of Jesus Christ of Latter-day Saints (LDS) in Kensington, Maryland, known as the Washington D.C. Temple.[7] The 18-foot golden statue on the highest eastern spire is of the angel Moroni, the angel who is said to have led prophet Joseph Smith in a series of visions beginning in 1823 to the golden plates that form the basis of the Book of Mormon. Begun in 1968 and opened in 1974, the temple in the shape of an elongated hexagon is a late modern interpretation of the famed Salt Lake Temple in Salt Lake City, Utah, the "most recognized symbol of the [LDS] Church" completed in 1893 (fig. 16).[8] Its two groups of three spires, symbolizing the Melchizedek and Aaronic Priest-hoods within Mormonism, directly reference the six-spire arrangement of the Salt Lake Temple. Significantly, the Washington D.C. Temple was the first modern-day Mormon temple east of the Mississippi. Its location just ten miles north of downtown Washington, D.C., the nation's political center of power, confirmed for some Mormonism's move

**Figure 15.** "SURRENDER DOROTHY" graffiti painted on bridge over the Capital Beltway in view of the Washington D.C. Temple in 1986. (United Press International)

"from a frontier religion to a major religion."[9] One of the temple's LDS architects,
Keith Wilcox, put the importance of the temple's location in weightier terms: referring to the fact that the Latter-day Saints were chased out of Ohio and Missouri in
the early nineteenth century, he claimed that the temple would "visually represent
the literal return of the Church to that part of the United States from whence it
was driven."[10] The temple—which differs from a Mormon church or meetinghouse
in the sacred rites that are preformed there and a much more restrictive rule about
who may enter it—was to serve the 300,000 LDS members then living east of the
Mississippi, in eastern Canada, and in the Caribbean in the 1970s as well as those
new members the LDS Church expected to gain in the decades to come.[11]

Yet in framing the building within *The Wizard of Oz* narrative and image, the
public—outsiders to the Mormon religion—co-opted the identity and purpose of

the temple in what art and religious historian Sally Promey has called "a form of editorial vandalism."[12] As Promey argues, "[public] display generates a discursive space, a social and political arena, where cultural negotiations about identities both individual and collective take place." Although "religious displays often seek to exercise control of interpretative possibilities by the inclusion of easily legible and widely recognizable symbols and images pared down to their most basic elements," the case of the Washington D.C. Temple is one where the LDS Church, the temple's owner and builder, could not control the reception of its symbols, nor did the public necessarily understand what these symbols were.[13]

The analogy of the Washington D.C. Temple to *The Wizard of Oz* is a way for the non-Mormon public (or publics) to make sense of a paradoxically inaccessible building, one everybody can see but only worthy Mormons can enter. While Mormons believe that the temple's restriction makes it "sacred, not secret," it nevertheless excludes this public from the experiences of the interior of the building, and its exterior Mormon symbols are also largely illegible to this non-Mormon public. By analogizing the building to *The Wizard of Oz,* the public creates an alternative narrative for it within a familiar and widely known popular culture story and image. But while humorous and witty, the analogy to *The Wizard of Oz* also denigrates the sacrality of the temple, casting it as a fiction and fantasy. In invoking the image of the "man behind the curtain"—the great and powerful Wizard of Oz who was proven to be a fraud—the analogy challenges the validity of Mormonism, playing on long-held prejudices and misunderstandings of Mormonism and undermining religious belief itself. The graffiti "SURRENDER DOROTHY" transforms the Washington D.C. Temple from a landscape of belief to a landscape of doubt, both playfully drawing on allusions to a popular culture icon and more darkly challenging the origins and theology of the LDS faith that the public—or a portion of the non-Mormon public—struggles to accept.

## Mormonism's Image in the Late Twentieth Century

In the 1960s and 1970s, The Church of Jesus Christ of Latter-day Saints engaged in an orchestrated public relations campaign to improve its public image. While the public—construed in its broadest sense—seemed to have high opinions of individual Mormons, known for their devotion to family, work, and "clean living" with abstinence from caffeine, tobacco, and alcohol, the public's opinion of the LDS Church as an institution was mixed. A 1973 LDS survey pinpointed "obscurity" rather than "opposition" to the Mormon church as the central challenge to a public understanding of Mormonism.[14] The public appeared to have "a general ignorance of LDS beliefs," including trouble identifying Mormonism as a Christian religion, a misunderstanding that continues today.[15] The issue of polygamy in the Mormon church, a practice leaders Joseph Smith and Brigham Young engaged in, which was formally disavowed by the church in 1890, continued to dog public opinion of Mormonism. Mormons were also caught up in the cultural politics of the time. The church's policy barring men of African descent from becoming priesthood holders—a policy that would not be changed until 1978—and its opposition to the Equal Rights Amendment to grant equal rights to women cast the church as racist and sexist in an era of intense civil rights struggles.[16]

Yet in other ways, the LDS Church succeeded in positively raising its public profile in the 1960s and 1970s. In politics, Michigan governor George Romney's 1968 bid for the Republican nomination for United States president put a Mormon candidate into the national spotlight. In popular culture, Mormon entertainers such as the Osmond family and the Mormon Tabernacle Choir were famous, well-liked figures.[17] To exert greater control of its public image, in 1972 the church created a Public Communications Department that conducted opinion polls about Mormonism and directed Mormon engagement in television and media.[18] The church's more active role in shaping, asserting, and controlling its message in the media appeared to pay off. A 1977 assessment in a LDS publication of Mormons' treatment in the press concluded that "in the 1970's the Church has been surprisingly successful in gaining recognition and media coverage on those aspects it would most like to have publicized—integrity, devotion to the Puritan work ethic, the family, genealogy, temples and proper health habits." The assessment also noted that the writers in the secular press "take their [Mormon] subjects more seriously than in the past" and that Mormon "events which in the past would have called forth derisiveness or flippancy now are treated with interest and insight."[19]

A milestone in the Mormons' attempt to actively cultivate a positive public image was the Mormon Pavilion at the 1964–65 New York World's Fair. Here, for the first time, the LDS Church created its own pavilion at a world's fair to proselytize its message, selecting a site at the main entrance to reach the highest number of fairgoers possible.[20] The pavilion's architecture was a conscious branding of Mormonism.[21] The entrance facade featured a near replica of the eastern front of the iconic neo-Gothic Salt Lake Temple positioned in front of an otherwise modernist structure (fig. 17). As architectural historian Julie Nicoletta has argued, "the replica temple façade applied to the bland building behind anticipates Robert Venturi's postmodern decorated shed." In appropriating the iconic image of the Mormon religion at the epicenter of the Mormon's realization of Zion on Earth, the Mormon Pavilion at the New York World's Fair through its very architecture "provided an occasion for visitors to learn about a religion that, until recently, had been associated with the West and remained mysterious to many Americans."[22] With displays edu-

**Figure 17.** The Pavilion of The Church of Jesus Christ of Latter-day Saints (center foreground) at the 1964 New York World's Fair by architect Harold Burton with a replica of the facade of the Salt Lake Temple at the entrance. (New York World's Fair 1964–1965 Corporation records, Manuscripts and Archives Division, The New York Public Library, Astor, Lenox, and Tilden Foundations)

cating fairgoers about Mormon beliefs and the short film *Man's Search for Happiness,* the pavilion attracted nearly 6 million of 50 million fairgoers. It was the second most visited religious pavilion at the fair behind the Vatican Pavilion and, from the viewpoint of the LDS Church, a highly successful outreach effort.[23]

### The Temple and Mormon Public Outreach

The success of the Mormon Pavilion at the 1964–65 New York World's Fair and the church's revamped public communications strategy played prominent roles in the creation of the Washington D.C. Temple, both in its architecture—the Washington D.C. Temple, for example, also explicitly referenced the Salt Lake Temple—and in how the temple was introduced to the public and the press. Before its dedication, the LDS Church opened the Washington D.C. Temple to the public for a six-week period from September 17 to November 2, 1974, with the intention of informing the public about the activities that were to take place in the temple and demystifying the LDS religion. Such open houses were and still are common practice for LDS temples, but these open houses are short-lived. Like all other Mormon temples, once the Washington D.C. Temple was dedicated during ceremonies spanning November 19 through November 22, 1974, it was only open to those Mormons in good standing with the church. Latter-day Saints must prove their worthiness to enter a temple in their adherence to Mormon practices, including keeping the Word of Wisdom (no alcohol, no caffeine, no smoking), regularly wearing temple garments under their clothing, and fully tithing to the church, and obtain a "temple recommend" from church leaders. A reported 758,328 visitors, including First Lady Betty Ford, took advantage of the opportunity to tour the Washington D.C. Temple during this open period. Notably, it was during the open house that the "SURRENDER DOROTHY" message first appeared.

That the LDS Church viewed the open house as a public relations opportunity was further underscored by a 15-question survey commissioned by the church's Public Communications Department and given to 2,100 visitors to the Washington D.C. Temple. This survey, whose findings were published in a 1975 report, gauged public knowledge and attitudes about the temple and the LDS Church and recorded the demographics of those curious about the temple. Ninety-five percent of those surveyed were not Mormon, and nearly 90 percent came from within a 100-mile radius of the temple.[24] The published report noted that more than a third of those surveyed understood that the temple was only to be used by Mormons for sacred ordinances.[25] Understood another way, the majority of visitors—nearly two-thirds of those surveyed—did not understand exactly what the temple's purpose was or that it was for the exclusive use of Mormons.

The survey findings suggested that the temple's architecture and siting resonated strongly with the public. Nearly 97 percent thought positively about the exterior, and nearly 92 percent felt the same about the interior.[26] A testimonial by one local visitor highlighted in the report demonstrated the temple building was doing the very work it was intended to do:

> I commute daily on the beltway on my way to work, approximately six o-clock a.m. every morning. I cannot express the feeling I get as I see the Mormon Temple appearing in the distance. To me it is the "Eighth Wonder of the World." Even though I am not of the Mormon Faith, I feel the presence of God every time I gaze upon this magnificent structure.[27]

Such a comment spoke to the temple's intentional location on the Beltway. The church acquired the large site in 1962, just as construction on the Beltway was underway (the highway was completed in 1964). Church publicity materials at the time of the temple's site dedication in 1968 emphasized the location's easy accessibility from the interstate, local airports, and also rail travel for those Mormons journeying to the temple. But the site also had a great publicity value because of all those who would see it from the highway. This was the intent: "We hope this design does attract a great deal of attention so that people will investigate the church."[28] As architect Keith Wilcox asked rhetorically, "Where better can we preach the message than down on the Beltway?"[29] As much as the temple was for the Latter-day Saints, it was also very much intended for a wider public.

The report painted an exceedingly optimistic portrait of the public's reception of the temple and the efficacy of the open house. It concluded, "The fact that more than three-quarters of a million visitors came to see the House of the Lord may be interpreted as a favorable sign and a recognition that The Church Of Jesus Christ of

Latter-day Saints is a major Christian denomination within the national pattern of religion."[30] Missing were any critical comments of the temple, which if not expressed by the survey respondents were nevertheless prominent in the press.

### The Washington D.C. Temple's Critical Reception

From the beginning, the Washington D.C. Temple was understood by critics as an amalgam of popular images rather than a product of elite taste.[31] *New York Times* architectural critic Paul Goldberger, who toured the temple during the 1974 open house, claimed that the building "probably comes closer to reflecting the architectural ideal of many Americans than do buildings of far more serious interest to architects." He denounced the building's design as "pedestrian," "very dull," and "of little real imagination." When the building did engage the imagination, it did so according to a popular conception of modernism. To Goldberger's eye, the building's "fantasy" and "almost Disneyland-like" exterior approximated not celebrated modern architecture, but "the awkward forms that were always supposed to indicate 'modern building' in old comic strips." Referencing Buck Rogers, a fictional character whose adventures in the imagined future were detailed in a popular comic strip, movies, and television series from the 1920s through the 1980s, Goldberger wrote that it seemed "as if the architects had tried to design Buck Rogers's church."[32] A writer in the *Washington Post* claimed that the building "resembles a couple of space shuttles on the launch pad as much as a feudal castle," further positioning the building as a Space Age structure.[33] Quite simply, the building, according to critics like Goldberger, presented a caricatured version of modernism as portrayed in American popular culture.

To these critics, the building's mismatched traditional interior proved just how much it failed true modernist design principles. For Goldberger, the interior "tries desperately to be 'good taste'—and if good taste consists of ringing a crystal chandelier with florescent lighting, then it succeeds."[34] Goldberger was not alone in this opinion. A Methodist minister named Gerald Forshey, writing in the *Christian Century,* agreed that the building was a study in popular, middle-class taste and a kaleidoscope of references. Like Goldberger, Forshey was able to tour the temple interior during the open house, and he made note of the "Mormon muzak" pumped through the speakers as visitors walked through the building. Of the massive baptismal font representing twelve marble oxen on a lower floor of the temple, Forshey quipped, "Cecil B. DeMille could have designed it." The atmosphere of the 1,600-seat Solemn Assembly Room on the seventh floor of the structure, the temple's largest room and rarely used, suggested to Forshey "a religious ballroom atop a Hilton hotel." The rich carpets, curtains, and traditional upholstered furniture rendered in whites and creams, baby blues and pinks, apricots and lemon yellows made Forshey feel "for a moment that I was in one of those elaborate funeral homes that resemble Howard Johnson's motel lobbies" (fig. 18).[35] Comparisons of the temple to hotel interiors were common, perhaps spurred by the knowledge that local hotelier and LDS member J. W. Marriott was a major financial contributor to the building. *Time* magazine noted the temple "with its thick carpets, pastel velour upholstery and soft lights, suggest a posh hotel more than a church," and Goldberger concurred: "The inside is a bizarre cross between a Holiday Inn and Forest Lawn [Cemetery]."[36] While Foshey's opinion piece was ultimately an indictment of scholars and other critics for their snobbery of these popular culture references, his account and Goldberger's nevertheless put front and center how the temple trafficked in these popular

**Figure 18.** Opulent interior of a sealing room, Washington D.C. Temple, 1974. [Photograph by Eldon Linschoten published in *[The Church of Jesus Christ of Latter-day Saints] Church News,* November 23, 1974, MS 22200 Deseret News Press [Corporation] photograph archives [prints], circa 1950–1990, box 69, folder "Temple, Washington, D.C. [Interior]," Church History Library, The Church of Jesus Christ of Latter-day Saints, Salt Lake City, Utah, courtesy of the Deseret News Publishing Company, Salt Lake City, Utah]

images. Even the experience of the open house was understood "as an amusement outing as much as a visit to a religious shrine."[37]

While an attack on architectural taste, the derisive accounts by those who toured the Washington D.C. Temple may have also stemmed from a lack of familiarity with Mormonism and particularly Mormon temple practices. The temples of The Church of Jesus Christ of Latter-day Saints are not used for regular worship meetings that take place each Sunday at Mormon meetinghouses or churches (both names are given to these regular worship spaces) and are open to anyone. By contrast, temples are used for special, sacred rites that occur more infrequently and again are restricted to "temple worthy" Mormons. The rites performed inside a Mormon temple include baptism; sealing ceremonies that emphasize bonds that last "for time and all eternity"; and sacred ordinances that educate Latter-day Saints about their role in the world and eternal life. Collectively, these rites are known as "temple work," and they are both for the living and, controversially, on behalf of the dead who could not engage in these rites.[38] Because the rituals of Mormons are unfamiliar, so too is the layout of Mormon temples, which defies typical expectations of religious spaces. Whereas we expect to find a large space on the main floor for community gathering comparable to a nave or auditorium, the Washington D.C. Temple is instead a warren of 294 rooms, most small in scale, scattered across seven floors (see fig. 20).[39] These rooms range from the functional—administrative offices, a kitchen, a nursery, and locker rooms—to the ceremonial—the baptism room, fourteen sealing rooms, six sacred ordinance rooms, and the double-height Celestial Room, a representation of heaven, which participants enter through a curtain (or veil) after receiving the sacred ordinances. Since temple practices are not publicly discussed, the misunderstandings of these spaces and their uses make them primed for satire and condescension from outsider critics.

Although critics perceived the Washington D.C. Temple as an odd amalgam of popular images, its Mormon architects put forward its design as an earnest creation of a sacred space. Hugh B. Brown, the First Counselor of the First Presidency in The Church of Jesus Christ of Latter-day Saints at the time, rejected "several nationally known architects" for the temple's design who could not seem to grasp the intricacies of LDS religious architecture.[40] Instead, the design was created by Mormon architects Fred L. Markham, Harold K. Beecher, Henry P. Fetzer, and Keith W.

Wilcox working out of their Salt Lake City offices. Wilcox's design scheme chosen for the temple had its genesis in his master's thesis at the University of Oregon, and he documented his divine inspiration for the Washington D.C. Temple in a published account subtitled "a personal testimonial." In this account, Wilcox laid out the objectives for the design, including the desire for the temple to have "a certain timeless quality, relating to the past, present and future" and to "[avoid] the popular 'style' of the day." Importantly, Wilcox believed that the "Temple should easily and immediately be recognized as a 'Mormon' Temple." He explained that it should reference the Salt Lake Temple, but he also stressed the Washington D.C. Temple should have "its own unique expression and form" rather than be a mere "copy."[41]

This drive for legibility of Mormonism through architecture, a principle stressed in the Mormon Pavilion at the New York World's Fair, was also in accord with an emerging postmodern architecture of the 1960s and 1970s. Although architect Keith Wilcox claimed to want to "[avoid] the popular 'style' of the day,'" his design for the Washington D.C. Temple was very much a part of the shift away from architectural modernism of the 1930s, 1940s, and 1950s—the modernist box of architects such as Ludwig Mies van der Rohe—and toward such designs as Philip Johnson's New York State Theater (now David H. Koch Theater) at Lincoln Center (1964) in New York City and Edward Durell Stone's John F. Kennedy Center for the Performing Arts (1971) in Washington, D.C., in a style known as New Formalism or Modern Classicism.[42] These buildings returned to more overt references to classicism, such as delicate columns, to create monumentality, but missing from this kind of architecture was the revolutionary vocabulary and forms of modernism. New Formalism was a way to reengage popular taste after an era of modernism that catered to elite sensibilities, as the editor of *Architectural Forum* Douglas Haskell claimed in the 1958 article "Architecture and Popular Taste."[43] Foreshadowing postmodernism, Haskell saw a "coming rapprochement between modern architecture and popular taste" and identified what he called "three popular desires" on the part of the public for architecture. The first was for "more decorativeness and romance than a highly intellectual architecture has been delivering"; the second, "for more drama: a 'good show,' symbolism, even fairy tales"; and the third, for "free improvisation in building design, newer rhythms, freshness and readiness in adaptation." Taken together, Haskell called these the desires for "the new romanticism, the new baroque, and the new improvisation" and in more colloquial terms "a trio of schmaltz, googie, and honky-tonk." Architects working within this popular taste in architecture described by Haskell included Eero Saarinen, Minoru Yamasaki, and Edward Durell Stone, whose work the design for the Washington D.C. Temple echoed. Their buildings celebrated, Haskell wrote, "the appearance in modern architecture of decorativeness, of symbolism, and of improvisation."[44] But not everyone believed this decoration and symbolism amounted to great architecture. As architecture critic Paul Goldberger wrote, referencing Stone's Kennedy Center in Washington, D.C., "Like its Washington neighbor, the Kennedy Center, the Mormon Temple has an ersatz sort of grandeur—it is a kind of para-architecture that has great pretensions but is at the bottom rather empty."[45]

In the quest to have the Washington D.C. Temple "easily and immediately be recognized as a 'Mormon' Temple," the temple architects played on Mormon symbolism associated with the Salt Lake Temple in ways that complemented emerging postmodern theory. Architectural theorists such as Charles Jencks in his 1977 book *The Language of Post-Modern Architecture* and Robert Venturi in the 1972 book *Learning from Las Vegas* with Denise Scott Brown and Steven Izenour assailed modernism as severe boxes that did not "speak" to the public. Jencks, Venturi, and other postmodernists sought to recover legible symbols, both those of the past and those in popular culture, for use in contemporary architecture.[46] The use of the Salt Lake Temple facade in the Mormon Pavilion in the 1964–65 World's Fair and references to the Salt Lake Temple for the Washington D.C. Temple engaged in this concept of legible symbols, as most religious structures attempt to do. For the Washington D.C. Temple, in addition to the inclusion of the angel Moroni statue and the arrangement of the six spires, the architects used the Gothic pointed arch motif throughout the complex—from doorknobs to the perimeter fence—in explicit reference to the Salt Lake Temple and to mark the building as "Mormon," even though the building itself, either on the exterior or interior, had little to do with Gothic Revival architecture. Critic Paul Goldberger understood this, though his comments were derisive. He said the Gothic arch details "suggest nothing so much as those corporate headquarters that endeavor to work their trademark into every possible aspect of their design—only here the trademark is Gothic architecture."[47]

Yet while these symbols and references were well understood by Latter-day

Saints, for the non-Mormon public this legibility was not as clear. To understand the identity of the Washington D.C. Temple without a written sign, non-Mormon viewers would have to know the Salt Lake Temple well enough to get the reference to it in the Washington D.C. Temple's spires, or they would have to know the importance of the angel Moroni to the Mormon story to understand the statue on one of its spires. This visual literacy of Mormonism was perhaps too much to expect of the public on the East Coast where Mormonism was not as prominent and since Mormonism remains a minority religion in the United States at under 2 percent of the population. Mormon symbols simply are not widely familiar. To make sense of the building, the public crafted an alternative narrative unanticipated by the temple architects.

## The Mormon Temple as Oz

For more than forty years, the non-Mormon public, via anonymous graffiti artists, has perpetuated the "SURRENDER DOROTHY" graffiti to explain the identity of the Washington D.C. Temple and the religious rites they are not allowed to witness. While the comparison between the temple and Oz appears simply as a moment of great wit playing off their formal similarities, the analogy is actually an apt exposition of the temple's characteristics when we fully unpack it. The analogy is also a more caustic religious satire of Mormonism when we understand it as the public's way to counter its exclusion from this sacred space. The comparison of the Washington D.C. Temple to *The Wizard of Oz* challenges The Church of Jesus Christ of Latter-day Saints and even religious belief itself in a fully realized landscape of doubt.

The public quickly gets the building's analogy to *The Wizard of Oz* because the Oz images are so familiar in American popular culture. The 1939 *The Wizard of Oz* movie, famous for actress Judy Garland's performance as Dorothy and televised nationally in an annual ritual from 1959 to 1991, is an ingrained part of the common American experience. Images of the Yellow Brick Road and the Emerald City; songs such as "Somewhere over the Rainbow" and "Follow the Yellow Brick Road"; characters such as Dorothy, Toto, the Wicked Witch of the West, the Lion, the Tin Man, and the Scarecrow; and Dorothy's famous ruby red slippers continue to permeate American culture. One pair of the ruby red slippers worn by Garland is displayed at the Smithsonian's National Museum of American History in Washington, D.C., as an iconic part of movie history and American material culture. Even if the narrative story of *The Wizard of Oz* is sometimes fuzzy in the American memory, the images of it are strong and clear.[48]

Because of this familiarity, the public can easily compare the Washington D.C. Temple to Oz at the suggestion of the "SURRENDER DOROTHY" graffiti. How the temple is revealed visually replicates how the Royal Palace of Oz appears in the movie: Dorothy and her friends first see the Royal Palace of Oz off in the distance as they walk along the Yellow Brick Road, just as drivers encounter the Washington D.C. Temple off in the distance from the vantage point of a highway. The Oz palace as a seat of power is conveyed in its massiveness, just as the temple in its size and location indicates a seat of power. Architecturally, the Oz palace of the movie stage set is a collection of vertical towers, in the same way that the six spires of the Mormon temple are its dominant feature. The obvious distinction between the Washington D.C. Temple and the Oz palace of the movie is that the temple is white while the Oz palace is green, the color of the Emerald City. (Here the Washington D.C. Temple tracks more closely to *The Wonderful Wizard of Oz* book, where the Oz palace was white—author L. Frank Baum may have been inspired by what he saw at the 1893 World's Columbian Exposition in Chicago with its famed white Court of Honor—and only appeared green because residents wore green-colored glasses.) Because the "SURRENDER DOROTHY" signage is a recognizable graffiti rather than an officially sanctioned marker, the public gets the joke that this building must be something other than Oz, but the analogy is obvious enough to provoke a smile from drivers on the Capital Beltway.

The analogy of the temple to Oz takes on greater poignancy and accuracy when we understand how the temple and Oz operate in the world. The Emerald City and the Washington D.C. Temple are both what Mircea Eliade called an *axis mundi,* an ordering center of the world and a connection point between the human and the divine.[49] As Eliade argues, almost anything can be an *axis mundi,* but pillars, trees, ladders, mountains, and other vertical elements are common precisely because of their height as the imagined connection between heaven above, Earth in the middle, and the underworld below. The Emerald City and the Palace of Oz are the locus of power in the Land of Oz, and the palace as visualized in the movie conveys this center in its great height and massiveness. Similarly, in outlining the principles for the Washington D.C. Temple's design, architect Keith Wilcox stated, "The Temple should visually express our relationship to God" in its "aspiring quality," which he argued resided in its seven-story massing and six spires.[50] The height of the temple itself is augmented by its location on a 90-foot hill, which sets up the building as the tallest monument in the area and further increases its visibility. The Mormon temple and the Oz palace are sacred spaces in the Eliade sense because they are points of interruption of the sacred into the profane, or ordinary, world. The Land of Oz is a place set apart (though not heaven itself) where magic is possible. Similarly, the Mormon temple and its 57-acre site, which Wilcox compared to the "Sacred Grove," is a sanctuary from the rest of the world with a promise of divine help, just as Dorothy believed Oz held the key to what she desired, and it has its own visualization of heaven in its Celestial Room. More than an *axis mundi,* we can also interpret the Emerald City and the Washington D.C. Temple as realizations of the promised City of God, also known as the New Jerusalem or the City of Zion. In building temples, churches, and communities, the Latter-day Saints were (and still are) engaged in realizing Zion to call forth the Second Coming of Christ.[51] The Washington D.C. Temple was part of this project. In its magical qualities, the Emerald City in *The Wizard of Oz* can be read as an analogy to this promised land, this Zion.[52]

To experience these sacred, protective spaces, both the temple and Oz require a journey with obstacles to overcome. Glinda the Good Witch of the North instructs Dorothy to follow the Yellow Brick Road to the Emerald City to find her way back home to Kansas. Along the way, Dorothy, Toto, and their companions the Scarecrow, the Lion, and the Tin Man encounter a field of deadly poppies created by the Wicked Witch of the West. Dorothy, Toto, and the Lion fall victims to the poppies' sleep-inducing powers before being rescued by Glinda. In a comparable way, temple visitors also encounter obstacles on their journey. The traffic and speed on the Capital Beltway make travel to the temple time-consuming and even dangerous, and once off the Beltway the paucity of signs pointing to the temple and the winding road up to it obscure the path. This difficult journey parallels the Mormon story. In the winter of 1846–47, Brigham Young led the Mormons across the United States to the Great Basin—the land that would become the state of Utah—enduring great hardships of severe weather and lack of food. Here we have a triple mirror: Dorothy's journey to the Emerald City mirrors the temple visitor's journey to find the temple, which mirrors the Mormons' journey to find their home in the American West, which is itself a mirror of the Jews' journey through the Egyptian desert. These journeys are liminal spaces that give time for contemplation of the destination and increase the distinction between the mundane world and the sacred. The difficulties in arriving at these sacred spaces heighten the experience of the sacred.

It is at this point of arrival that the comparisons of the temple to Oz diverge, for while Oz is accessible, the temple is not. Dorothy knocks on the gates of Oz to seek entrance, and while she is at first denied, she and her companions are eventually allowed inside. Visitors who go up to the Washington D.C. Temple find a similarly controlled gate, but here, as *Time* magazine noted, "the curious outsider invariably meets a closed door" despite the fact that the temple's architecture explicitly draws visitors.[53] The inaccessible temple creates profound curiosity. As one neighbor said in 1981, "All I wonder is what's in there. I pass by. I stare at it everyday. At night I see it out my window, but I can't get in. I'd pay money to go inside."[54] Anthropologist Mark Leone characterized the temple in its restriction this way: "[The temple] is a massively confusing paradox: it is not identified, its use is secret, it is a closed magnet in the sense that it draws but it does not draw inside; it tempts but does not satisfy."[55]

The public overcomes the temple's secrecy and restriction by perpetuating the analogy to Oz, forming an alternative identity for the building as Oz itself. By recasting the building as the Palace of Oz via the "SURRENDER DOROTHY" graffiti, the public can imagine its interior, its rituals, and its people via the images in *The Wizard of Oz* movie. The building in this sense is no longer a Mormon temple but the actual Oz palace itself—the real, physical realization of a fantasy story embedded in the American memory. The building locates our desire for the supernatural and a world of the "other" much as the way Cinderella Castle in the Magic Kingdom in Walt Disney World makes childhood fantasy real in the material, physical world. In this sense of the Washington D.C. Temple as Oz and a realization of fantasy, the analogy is at its gentlest. It is not satire, but rather an expression of our desires for the fantastical.

The analogy of the Washington D.C. Temple to *The Wizard of Oz* becomes darkly satirical when we interpret the analogy as casting the Mormon faith as false—an interpretation that hinges on the comparison of Joseph Smith, the founder of the LDS faith, to the Wizard of Oz. In the movie, when Dorothy and her companions first see the Wizard of Oz, they are presented with the image of a gigantic floating head with no body whose booming voice terrifies them. The source of the wizard's power resides in this fearful image and also in the fact that he does not appear to many people. As the Wizard of Oz states in the book, "Usually I will not see even my subjects, and so they believe I am something terrible."[56] When Dorothy and her companions return to the wizard after fulfilling their mission to kill the Wicked Witch of the West, Toto famously pulls back the curtain to reveal the real wizard is a mere man controlling a machine-manufactured image of a terrifying wizard. The real Wizard of Oz admits that he is a "humbug," a term for a dishonest person.[57] Since the nineteenth century, the belief that Joseph Smith was also a charlatan has persisted. As early as 1838, a New York social critic called Joseph Smith "the most shocking humbug."[58] For these skeptics of Mormonism, Joseph Smith invented a religion with wild claims about being visited by supernatural beings and suspect practices such as faith healing. For them, Joseph Smith had no real power or connection to the divine, just like the Wizard of Oz. In *The Wizard of Oz,* the wizard sends Dorothy to kill the Wicked Witch of the West, something he himself cannot do. Furthermore, despite his promises, he does not return Dorothy back to Kansas, ultimately flying away in his hot air balloon without her, and he cannot really award that which the Scarecrow, the Lion, and the Tin Man seek either.[59] In the analogy of Joseph Smith to the Wizard of Oz, drawing back the curtain on what was secret reveals a fraud. The analogy suggests that the secret Mormon temple houses fraudulent claims about faith made by Joseph Smith and The Church of Jesus Christ of Latter-day Saints.

The satirizing of the Washington D.C. Temple and Mormonism as fraudulent belief draws its power from long-standing suspicions, prejudices, and biases about Mormonism. In his study of anti-Mormonism in the nineteenth century, historian J. Spencer Fluhman situates the convictions "that Joseph Smith was a charlatan, that Mormon religious practice was little more than delirium or occult magic, that Mormon theology amount[ed] to a thinly veiled moneymaking scheme, or that Mormon community building was a menacing empire-in-the-making" within a larger context of Protestant anxieties that the foundational value of religious disestablishment could lead to the rise of false religions.[60] For some, Mormonism is a religion invented less than two hundred years ago in the 1820s, not in the Holy Land in the Middle East but in western New York State, by a man named Joseph Smith, not Jesus Christ. While Latter-day Saints do use the Old and New Testaments of the accepted Bible in the Judeo-Christian tradition, the Book of Mormon—the so-called restored Gospel found buried by Joseph Smith in New York State as claimed by the Mormons—seems an invention of Smith's imagination rather than a revealed scripture. Some also do not believe the Book of Mormon's claim that Jewish tribes emigrated to the Americas as early as 600 BC, making Latter-day Saints of the tribes of Israel. Suspicions of Mormons are as much cultural as they are theological. Some see Mormonism as a cult or ethnic group rather than a religion, based on the perception that Mormons are an insular group who give preferential treatment to other Mormons in the secular world. The Mormons' white undergarments, worn under normal clothing as a sign of fidelity, remain a source of curiosity and derision even though special clothing is part of other religions, as in the hijab and burka of Islam.[61] Mormons' practice of early marriage, relatively early and frequent childbirth among Mormon women, and the fact that women cannot be priesthood holders in the LDS Church also raise questions for some about women's empowerment within the religion. The analogy of the Washington D.C. Temple to *The Wizard of Oz* capitalizes on these suspicions of and disagreements with Mormon belief, practices, and culture. In aligning the Mormon religion with images of flying monkeys, magic shoes, lions who talk, and scarecrows who come alive, the analogy makes an overt mockery of Mormonism as a fiction.

Moreover, the analogy of the Washington D.C. Temple and Mormonism to *The Wizard of Oz* attacks the notion that religion can give us something that we do not already possess. While the Wizard of Oz gives symbolic mementos—a medal for the Lion's courage, a diploma for the Scarecrow's brain, a heart-shaped mechanism for the Tin Man's heart—the truth is that they already possessed courage, intelligence, and a kind heart as proven in their journey with Dorothy. Dorothy had the power all along to return home by clicking her ruby slippers (silver slippers in the book) and saying, "There's no place like home." Dorothy also has power to defeat evil herself, as when she kills the Wicked Witch of the West by throwing water on her (even if accidently). One lesson of *The Wizard of Oz* is belief in the inner self and our own capabilities. When we apply this lesson to our real world, as the "SURRENDER DOROTHY" graffiti prompts us to do, the conclusion is that we do not need to rely on or appeal to a higher power for salvation. This idea of faith and religion as hollow is the heart of the satirical recasting of the Washington D.C. Temple as Oz.

Finally, the analogy of the Washington D.C. Temple to Oz is a commentary on the involuntary nature of encountering religion in public. Dorothy did not ask to visit the Land of Oz (even though she tried to run away from home) but was whisked away there by a tornado. Similarly, the encounter of the D.C. Temple is also involuntary. We the public do not explicitly ask to see it. Rather, we are confronted with its image as we drive along the Beltway in the course of other activities. But once confronted, we must make sense of it. The "SURRENDER DOROTHY" graffiti is a way to make sense of the Washington D.C. Temple, to locate it within a readily identifiable cultural image, and to overcome what is ultimately a baffling paradox of seeing a very public image with a very private use.

### Mormon Response to "Surrender Dorothy"

The Church of Jesus Christ of Latter-day Saints is well aware of the long-standing "SURRENDER DOROTHY" graffiti outside its Washington D.C. Temple. The *Deseret News,* a newspaper owned by The Church of Jesus Christ of Latter-day Saints published in Salt Lake City, included a 2011 article with the headline "The D.C. Temple Graffiti Prank Won't Die" and in a 1989 article acknowledged that the temple "does look somewhat like the movie version of the city of Oz." These accounts stressed the gentle interpretation of the analogy of the temple to Oz, writing that the temple was "known affectionately by locals as Oz" and emphasizing that the analogy was in the spirit of "a sense of fun" rather than a more caustic religious satire.[62] In this acknowledgment of the existence of the graffiti and the framing of the narrative in harmless terms, the church seeks to disarm the power of the graffiti.

The LDS Church attempts to counter the idea of its temples' inaccessibility and secrecy through its temple visitors' centers. As one Washington D.C. Temple administrator reasoned in 2001, "When they don't know you, people seem to think you resemble Oz. That's why we have a visitor's [*sic*] center."[63] The creation of visitors' centers at Mormon temples and sites of historic importance came directly from the success of the Mormon Pavilion at the 1964–65 New York World's Fair, though they had roots in Bureaus of Information in the early twentieth century.[64] Mormon leaders understood from the fair the outreach potential of a building dedicated to teaching the public about the Mormon faith. The first official visitors' center was added to the Salt Lake Temple Square in 1966, with plans for a visitors' center at the Washington D.C. Temple outlined two years later in 1968, conceived as a part of the temple precinct from the beginning. The Salt Lake City and D.C. visitors' centers drew on much from the New York pavilion. Like the New York pavilion, the two centers prominently display the *Christus* statue, a replica of the 1821 statue of a resurrected Jesus Christ by sculptor Bertel Thorvaldson located in Copenhagen, to immediately dispel any doubt that Mormons believe in eternal salvation through Christ. Both the Salt Lake and D.C. centers also showed the film *Man's Search for Happiness,* created for the New York fair. Films, multimedia exhibits, photographs, performances, and volunteer missionaries who engage visitors in conversations about the LDS faith are common parts of the Mormon visitors' center experience. If the temple exterior draws the public, the visitors' center actively engages a public not able to enter the temple itself.

But the Mormon temple visitors' centers are not a substitute for the temple experience itself. Architecturally, these centers are banal in comparison to the temple architecture — often one or two stories in contrast to the tall temple, with no ornament — and are clearly secondary spaces to the main event (fig. 19). To compensate for the lack of access to the temple, the centers employ devices to approximate the temple experience. At the D.C. center, a large glass wall directs the visitors' gaze toward the temple's entrance facade. In 2015, the D.C. visitors' center added a cutaway architectural model of the temple (also at the visitors' centers in Salt Lake City and Rome) as part of a larger public relations effort at making the temples and their rituals more visible (fig. 20). The model is located in front of the glass wall so that visitors simultaneously view the model and full-scale temple. It details the temple interior in miniature, replicating the furniture, lighting, interior colors, and ceremonial spaces. Because the model is an architectural section, visitors are able to gain an understanding of how the warren of spaces relate to each other across

**Figure 19.** Exterior of the Visitors' Center at the Washington D.C. Temple in 1976. (Photograph published in *[The Church of Jesus Christ of Latter-day Saints] Church News,* July 10, 1976, MS 22200 Deseret News Press [Corporation] photograph archives [prints], circa 1950–1990, box 69, folder "Temple, Washington, D.C. [Visitor's (*sic*) Center]," Church History Library, The Church of Jesus Christ of Latter-day Saints, Salt Lake City, Utah, courtesy of the Deseret News Publishing Company, Salt Lake City, Utah)

seven floors, an experience not possible when walking through the temple itself. This model and the accompanying photographs of the baptismal font, the sealing rooms, the sacred ordinance rooms, and the Celestial Room in a nearby display seem to give maximum transparency to the temple, revealing it visually and demystifying these spaces. Yet such a virtual tour is not a substitute for the real encounter of the temple. These representations of the interior cannot convey the phenomenological experience of walking through the temple's spaces; physically sensing their scale; experiencing the unveiling of one space unto another; hearing music, hushed voices, and silence; smelling the atmosphere; feeling the texture of the upholstery and carpets underfoot; and seeing the amber-color light as it streams through the building's thin Alabama marble cladding. More importantly, these displays do not depict Mormons undergoing their rituals and rites—living and practicing their

**Figure 20.** Cutaway model of the Washington D.C. Temple located in the Temple Visitors' Center, with a view of the full-size temple in the background. (Photograph by Margaret M. Grubiak)

religion. The visitor sees representations of empty rooms and cannot witness the ceremonies that occur, understand the number of people at each event, see their special garments, or hear the dialogue that unfolds. Photographs and architectural models simply cannot convey the feeling and experience of the sacred, both in terms of space and ritual. The visitors' center itself does not feel like a sacred space—it is a place of information, not worship. The fact that visitors cannot enter the temple means that they are shut out from the experience of the sacred.

MONUMENTAL JESUS

Although Mormons state that their temples are "sacred, not secret" as a way to explain their restriction and temper suspicion about their religion, such a rationale does not satisfy a public curious about these sacred spaces. In practice, the temple and its rites *are* secret to a non-Mormon public, and the temple visitors' center, despite its attempts at transparency, remains a poor substitute for the experience of the temple itself. The "SURRENDER DOROTHY" graffiti near the Washington D.C. Temple subversively challenges the sacred and secret nature of the temple, opening it up for an imagined democratic inclusion that is not actually possible.

The "SURRENDER DOROTHY" graffiti outside the Washington D.C. Temple operates on multiple levels. It wittily plays on the visual similarities of the temple to the Palace of Oz in an understanding of architecture by analogy. It also attempts to make sense of an inaccessible building, locating it instead in the widely known images of *The Wizard of Oz*. But the graffiti is also more a more caustic satire that reveals some Americans' anxieties about the Mormon faith. By suggesting that the Mormon religion is fraudulent, just as we come to find out that the great Wizard of Oz was merely a man behind the curtain, the graffiti recasts the temple as a landscape of doubt. The Mormon temple is both a landscape of faith—a sincere assertion of Mormon faith and theology—and a landscape of doubt where architectural reception transforms meaning. Both landscapes put questions about faith on inescapable public display, demanding Mormon and non-Mormon publics to confront what we believe.

# 3

## ADVENTURES IN THE EVANGELICAL THEME PARK

In the long-running satirical animated sitcom *The Simpsons,* Ned Flanders is the earnest, honest, and very Christian neighbor of the Simpson family in the everywhere town of Springfield, USA.[1] Ned is steadfast in his belief, most of the time: he avoids curse words (most of the time); he carries pieces of the true cross; he says prayers at meals and at night; and he reads biblical stories to his sons, Rod and Todd. But Ned is also fully human. He sometimes has a temper, and he sometimes struggles with his faith as he tries to understand the reason for evil and misfortune in the world.[2] Ned's fallibility as he lives out a life of Christian virtues in a culture at times hostile to them provides a key drama in the show. In the character of Ned Flanders, *The Simpsons* crafts a nuanced and sympathetic portrait of the American evangelical, but it also uses Ned to satirize evangelical belief as it operates within a broader American culture. As sociologist David Feltmate argues, "*The Simpsons'* depictions of religion matter because they are treated not as frivolous cartoon humor, but as satires which criticize competing moral and civic perspectives of religion's relevance in the United States."[3]

To paint the picture of Ned Flanders as an evangelical Christian and simultaneously satirize American evangelicalism, *The Simpsons* connects Ned to places of real Christian cultural space. We learn in *The Simpsons* that Ned is a graduate of

Oral Roberts University, a conservative Pentecostal university in Tulsa, Oklahoma, founded by televangelist Oral Roberts in 1963. We see Ned's Oral Roberts University diploma hanging in his house in a 1993 *Simpsons* episode.[4] The diploma itself becomes the object of humor as Homer Simpson attempts to co-opt the rights of a college degree simply by crossing out Ned's name and replacing it with his own. In *The Simpsons Uncensored Family Album* published by *Simpsons* creator Matt Groening in 1991, we see a postcard sent by Ned to the Simpson family with the title "Verbal Johnson's Praying Hands" and subtitle "America's Most Judgemental Religious Theme Park!" over an image of a giant sculpture of hands in the gesture of prayer (fig. 21).[5] The postcard's words are a tongue-in-cheek reference to Oral Roberts University in its substitution of the synonym "Verbal" for "Oral" and the common surname "Johnson" for the common surname "Roberts" as well as a biting critique of Roberts's conservative values in the "America's Most Judgemental Religious Theme Park!" tagline. The postcard's visualization of "praying hands" was a direct nod to the giant *Healing Hands* (1980) statue that now stands at the entrance to Oral Roberts University (fig. 22).[6]

Jim and Tammy Faye Bakker's Heritage USA theme park also makes an appear-

**Figure 21.** "Verbal Johnson's Praying Hands" postcard from Ned Flanders to the Simpsons, satirizing Oral Roberts University. (Reprinted from *The Simpsons Uncensored Family Album* by Matt Groening, © 1991 Matt Groening Productions, Inc; published by Harper Perennial; The Simpsons TM & © Twentieth Century Fox Film Corporation; All rights reserved)

**Figure 22.** *The Healing Hands* (1980) sculpture by Leonard D. McMurry at the main entrance to Oral Roberts University, Tulsa, Oklahoma, originally located at the base of the City of Faith. (Stephen Saks Photography/Alamy Stock Photo)

ance by analogy in *The Simpsons*. In the 2001 episode "I'm Goin' to Praiseland," we witness Ned carry out the wishes of his dead wife Maude in building a Christian theme park. The episode's writers based Praiseland on Pentecostal televangelists Jim and Tammy Faye Bakker's Heritage USA, a 2,300-acre Christian theme park in Fort Mill, South Carolina—just miles outside of Charlotte, North Carolina—opened in 1978 and closed in 1989 after the downfall of the Bakkers' Praise the Lord (PTL) empire due to sexual scandal and financial fraud (fig. 23). While the kind of Christian theme park that Ned builds with representations of Golgotha, the Garden of Eden, and King Solomon's Temple is more biblically literal than the theme park the Bakkers constructed, it was not far off. Jim Bakker had planned a full-scale Old Jerusalem theme park as well as a roller coaster through heaven and hell for Heritage USA, though neither was ever constructed.[7]

In connecting Oral Roberts University and Heritage USA to Ned Flanders, *The Simpsons* satirizes the idea of the evangelical theme park. Both Heritage USA and Oral Roberts University were indeed theme parks, though of different but related stripes. Jim and Tammy Faye Bakker constructed an evangelical theme park on the model of Disney, complete with a carousel, miniature train, and water park, which became the third most visited theme park in the United States behind Disneyland and Disney World in the 1980s. The Oral Roberts University campus was, as *The Simpsons* satirical postcard of "Verbal Johnson's Praying Hands" pointed out, a theme park itself, not one with a miniature golf course but one explicitly fashioned after the 1962 Seattle World's Fair and transformed into a permanent religious world's fair. The evangelical theme park was a real phenomenon, but its meaning read differently to different audiences.

**Figure 23.** Map of Jim and Tammy Faye Bakker's Heritage USA, Fort Mill, South Carolina, ca. 1986. (From www.theme parkbrochures.net /maps/heritage-usa/)

The evangelical theme park posited the question: Can God, and religion, be fun? For Pentecostals, the answer to this question was a resounding yes. The fusion of religion and entertainment was part of a strategy in the gathering of believers into the tent. As Jim Bakker said in reference to his water park at Heritage USA, "People ask me why a Christian complex needs a water park. Well, if the Bible says we are to be fishers of men, then the water park is just the bait. And I don't seen [sic] anything wrong in using some pretty fancy bait."[8] For evangelicals, trafficking in secular entertainment for religious ends was no contradiction: it co-opted secular culture with a religious message to increase the reach of the Gospel. As R. Laurence Moore wrote, "Bakker advertised Heritage USA to Christian families as the ultimate in a pleasurable vacation. They did not have to forgo any of the things that their non-Christian neighbors enjoyed. Bakker gave the Pentecostal emphasis on joy frank commercial expression."[9] This co-opting of popular culture was reflective of Pentecostals' worldview of God's immanence in everything, including believers' leisure time and economic lives. In his study of the Ark Encounter theme park in Kentucky, James Bielo outlines the ways that the evangelical and fundamentalist theme park trafficked in "immersive play" and entertainment for the purposes of conversion (see chapter 4).[10]

The evangelical theme park was the physical locus of the intermingling of religion and money, a core feature of American televangelism as it saturated American culture in the 1970s and 1980s. Televangelists advocated the "prosperity gospel," preaching that God wants "health and wealth" for his followers.[11] Oral Roberts's Pentecostal belief in faith healing was a core part of his evangelical ministry and his adherence to the prosperity gospel, leading him to build the City of Faith medical complex at his university. Roberts and the Bakkers raised enormous sums of money over the airways and satellite networks in order to perpetuate television, radio, and satellite broadcasts to spread the Gospel to the far corners of the Earth. But such fundraising also became self-enrichment for these televangelists. Oral Roberts, who grew up in poverty in rural Oklahoma, became a person with a Cadillac, country club memberships, and a televangelical enterprise worth millions of dollars. Jim and Tammy Faye spent well above their means, with luxury cars, vacation homes, boats, designer clothing—all of which came crashing down as it was revealed Jim Bakker embezzled funds from his Praise the Lord network. These images of wealth intermixed with religion were not only part of the fulfillment of the "health and wealth" gospel but also the circular path of evangelical fundraising and growth. Oral Roberts crafted his university campus in order to exude an image of prosperity and attract middle-class students.[12] The Bakkers used the buildings at Heritage USA—promising free stays at the luxurious Heritage Grand Hotel—to attract donors to the PTL. As Moore claimed, "Heritage USA and the PTL were efforts to make money by selling religion, but they were not, for all that, merely exploitative."[13] For these evangelicals, capitalism and religion could coexist easily and without contradiction.

But to outsiders and even some insiders, televangelism's conflation of religion with entertainment and money seemed sacrilegious. Aspects of Pentecostal theology—including faith healing, speaking in tongues, and prophecy—seemed unbelievable. Together, money, entertainment, and supernatural encounters proved fertile ground for religious satire. Heritage USA and Oral Roberts University offer us examples of these satires grounded in Christian cultural space and image. A 1987 photograph of the Reverend Jerry Falwell's plunge down Heritage USA's waterslide focused Falwell's own discomfort between the alliance of entertainment and religion in an example of an internal satire. *The Simpsons* episode "I'm Goin' to Praiseland" based on Heritage USA satirized the idea that learning about theology can actually be fun, countering the very premise of an evangelical theme park, and called into question central tenets of Pentecostal theology. A poster imagining a sign of a "900-FT JESUS X-ING" outside of the City of Faith at Oral Roberts University mocked Roberts's vision of a 900-foot Jesus that Roberts promoted to obtain donations. The Prayer Tower at Oral Roberts University was the place Roberts sequestered himself amid another claim in 1987 that "God would call me home" if he did not raise money for the City of Faith, a claim that was roundly mocked in a *Doonesbury* cartoon. In these reactions, Heritage USA and Oral Roberts University were recast from landscapes of faith to landscapes of doubt.

## The Evangelical Draw to the Theme Park

The fusion of entertainment and religious message has long been a mainstay of American evangelicalism. In the 1830s at the Western Museum in Cincinnati, Ohio, artist Hiram Powers sculpted thirty life-sized wax figures depicting Dante's *Inferno,*

**Figure 24.** Bird's-eye view of the Jerusalem Exhibit, 1904 Louisiana Purchase Exposition, St. Louis, Missouri. (From Anna F. Mamreo and Jerusalem Exhibit Company, *World's Fair Souvenir Album of Jerusalem: St. Louis, Mo., U.S.A., 1904* [St. Louis: Towers & Company, 1903], courtesy of the San Francisco Theological Seminary Library, San Francisco)

complete with a reported animatronic Satan.[14] Re-creations of the Holy Land are versions of the evangelical theme park.[15] In the 1870s, the Christian campground Chautauqua in New York crafted a miniaturized "Palestine Park," an imagined geography of the Holy Land that visitors could walk through and explore.[16] For the 1904 St. Louis World's Fair, Chicago architects Watson and Hazleton designed a sprawling Jerusalem exhibit at full scale (fig. 24).[17] The Holy Land USA theme park in Waterbury, Connecticut, which opened in 1960, rebuilt landmarks from Bethlehem and Jerusalem to physically re-create biblical stories.[18] In the twentieth century, secular entertainment culture played prominently in evangelical spaces. Pentecostal preacher Aimee Semple McPherson shamelessly engaged in Hollywood tactics in her elaborate productions to illustrate the Gospel in her Angelus Temple in Los Angeles in the 1920s.[19] In nearby Garden Grove, California, in the late 1950s, the Reverend Robert Schuller of the Reformed Church held his early Sunday services in the local drive-in theater by preaching from the concession stand roof. In 1961, architect Richard Neutra formalized this co-opting of entertainment for religious purposes with a walk-in, drive-in church for Schuller's congregation.[20] Oral Roberts employed Hollywood producers for his immensely popular quarterly religious television specials filmed at Oral Roberts University, interweaving superstar singers and celebrities with his religious message in variety shows that earned Emmy nominations for their production value. America's first Passion play—a reenactment of the Passion of Christ performed by actors and live animals on elaborate Holy Land stage sets—took place in 1968 at Gerald L. K. Smith's theme park in Eureka Springs, Arkansas, a tradition that continues today (see chapter 5). The Passion play was also a central feature of entertainment and religious instruction at Heritage USA. The Holy Land Experience in Orlando, Florida, which opened in 2001, perpetuates this reenactment of Christ's life as both theological instruction and entertainment. Timothy Beal's *Roadside Religion* is a travelogue of such places of roadside religious attractions in America that similarly fuse entertainment and belief.[21]

The creation of the modern evangelical theme park in the twentieth century was part of a wider movement by Protestant evangelicals to build complexes and campuses to locate the so-called electronic church, the collection of radio airways, satellite signals, and now internet technologies used by evangelicals to spread the Gospel to the world. Even as evangelicals aggressively employed broadcast technology and innovated it, their impulse to locate electronic church ministries in real space and time and provide a pilgrimage point for their followers persisted. These evangelicals built large-scale, multibuilding, multifunctional complexes as the physical headquarters of their electronic ministries. Heritage USA was home to Jim and Tammy Faye Bakker's PTL network as well as their worship spaces, hotels, a shopping mall, and entertainment facilities. University campuses also became a particularly popular forum for these televangelical headquarters: Oral Roberts constructed Oral Roberts University in Tulsa, Oklahoma (founded in 1963); Jerry Falwell, Liberty University in Lynchburg, Virginia (founded as a college in 1971 and granted university status in 1984); Pat Robertson, Regent University in Virginia Beach, Virginia (founded in 1977 as Christian Broadcasting Network University); and Jimmy Swaggart, Jimmy Swaggart Bible College in Baton Rouge, Louisiana (opened in 1984). Jim Bakker even proposed a university for Heritage USA.[22] The visible presence of large, white satellite dishes on these campuses underscored that the higher education was only one part of the evangelical drive to spread the Gospel to as large an audience as possible. The evangelical complex became a calling card and even status symbol for these televangelists. The evangelical theme park in particular was one version of the many ways evangelicals sought to reify the electronic church.

The evangelical theme park drew inspiration from the tradition of world's fairs, which began in the mid-nineteenth century and enjoyed popularity into the mid-twentieth century. World's fairs provided a template of how to fuse popular entertainment with educational messages and create sites for pilgrimage. Oral Roberts crafted his university campus as a permanent religious world's fair inspired by his visit to the 1962 Seattle World's Fair grounds. While holding a crusade on the Seattle fairgrounds some seven months after the fair had closed, Roberts saw the United States Science Pavilion by architect Minoru Yamasaki and the famed Seattle Space Needle. Roberts, working with his architects, would pattern buildings on his campus in the style of Yamasaki, and his 200-foot Prayer Tower drew inspiration from the Seattle Space Needle (see figs. 33, 34). The Prayer Tower also recalled the observation towers of Philip Johnson's New York State Pavilion at the 1964–65 New York World's Fair. For Heritage USA, Jim and Tammy Faye Bakker imagined a building directly inspired by the 1851 Great Exhibition in London. In the 1980s, they proposed an astounding one-million-square-foot Ministry Center with a 30,000-seat church sanctuary (never constructed) blatantly patterned after Joseph Paxton's Crystal Palace.[23] The prominent pavilions, arched window frames, and repetitious use of glass and steel mimicked Paxton's exterior design. In their architectural alliance with world's fairs forms, both Oral Roberts University and Heritage USA crafted environments to draw people into the physical world of their electronic churches and to fuse entertainment with their evangelical message.

The gold standard of American theme parks—Disneyland in Anaheim, California (opened 1955), and Walt Disney World in Orlando, Florida (opened 1971)—also proved to be irresistible inspiration and analogy for the evangelical theme park. Journalists called Oral Roberts University "an educational and spiritual Disneyland" as a way to convey some understanding of its fantastic and unusual architecture, which perhaps had most in common with Disneyland's Tomorrowland in its futuristic image.[24] For Heritage USA, Jim and Tammy Faye Bakker themselves cultivated a direct tie with Disney. The Bakkers visited Disneyland and Disney World regularly, and they were enamored with the parks. (Tammy Faye would even move to Orlando after the PTL scandals.) As Tammy Faye said,

> I have been to many places, but if my Utopia could look any way I wanted it to look, I'd like it to look like Disneyland. I love Disneyland, and if I could, I'd have the whole world look like Disneyland. The first time I walked into Disneyland I was so overwhelmed I started to cry. I mean, I just couldn't believe that there was any place as wonderful as Disneyland: wonderful houses, architecture, and bright colors. It's such a happy, sun-shiny place.[25]

Jim Bakker took the Disney parks as a literal design direction for Heritage USA. The green wrought iron fence that encircled Heritage USA echoed Disney's green wrought iron fence; Heritage USA's Fort Heritage campground echoed Disney's Fort Wilderness campground; and Heritage USA's Main Street with its Victorian-style storefronts echoed Disney's Main Street, USA with its Victorian-style storefronts. Heritage USA's carousel, miniature train, and later castle (planned by Bakker but constructed after his tenure) furthered the ties between the Disney parks and Heritage USA.[26] Disney also served as a business model for the Bakkers. Just like Disney's expansion from the original Disneyland in California to Disney World in Florida (and now parks in France, Japan, and China), the Bakkers also sought to franchise their park with a Heritage USA West in California, a project that never materialized.[27] Disney proved a readily accessible template that Jim Bakker simply followed to create his theme park. As Charles Shepard, a *Charlotte Observer* reporter who wrote Pulitzer Prize–winning articles on the PTL scandal and later a biography of Jim Bakker, observed, "Bakker may have been a creative mastermind, as most around him believe, but he was not an especially original thinker. Instead, he adapted secular commercial successes to his Christian world."[28] Bakker's mimicry of Disney paid off. In an often-cited statistic, by 1986 Heritage USA was the third most-visited theme park in the United States behind only Disneyland and Disney World, though Disneyland's reported 12.5 million visitors and Disney World's reported 15 million visitors in 1986 outshined Heritage USA's 6 million visitors.[29]

The idea that a theme park—whether Heritage USA and Oral Roberts University or Disneyland and Disney World—could be conceived of as a sacred space is not as farfetched as may first appear. Jim Bakker himself understood the blurred line between the sacred and the profane in regard to Disney: "Why is that we can almost enshrine a mouse, a Mickey Mouse or a Donald Duck? I mean, you hear the Mouseketeers' song . . . it's almost sung like a hymn."[30] Scholars have applied University of Chicago religious historian Mircea Eliade's concept of sacred space to the seemingly secular space of a theme park.[31] Disney World, for example, operates as a place set apart from the everyday with its own sense of sacred time. Visitors can reach the Magic Kingdom only by railway or crossing a lake by boat, a physical entry sequence that separates the park from the everyday and creates a moment of liminality, or condition between two worlds. The park itself, in its hyperreality and pristine image (all work performed by employees to keep the park clean and operational is hidden from visitors' view), can become magical to visitors. We can think of Disney World's highest peaks—including Cinderella Castle and Space Mountain—as an *axis mundi,* or center of the earth that connects heaven to earth. Heritage USA and Oral Roberts University also traffic in these spatial concepts of the sacred.[32] Visitors to Heritage USA entered the park via a half-mile drive into a forest, enacting a liminal space and casting the space of the park as different than the space of the everyday. Some visitors understood this qualitative difference in the space of Heritage USA, with some calling it "Heaven on earth."[33] At Oral Roberts University, the Prayer Tower operates as a clear *axis mundi,* connecting human endeavors to the divine through a physical tower of prayer. Just as Disneyland and Disney World draw millions of pilgrims each year, so too did Heritage USA and Oral Roberts University draw their own pilgrims. In 1969, a Kentucky steel mill worker and his wife drove to Tulsa specifically to visit Oral Roberts University. Their chance encounter with Oral Roberts himself on the campus became "the thrill of their vacation."[34] This understanding of an evangelical theme park—as something that could serve both as a space set apart that invokes divine connections and as entertainment—makes sense of the marrying of "evangelical" to "theme park."

## Heritage USA as a Landscape of Faith

When Jim and Tammy Faye Bakker broke ground for Heritage USA in Fort Mill, South Carolina, on January 2, 1978 (Jim Bakker's birthday), they set off on the creation of a 2,300-acre playground that encompassed all of their ministries and interests. For Jim Bakker, the idea of "church" was not just a singular building and its associated activities but rather a pervasive whole touching all parts of life: "Heritage Village Church [the umbrella organization of Heritage USA] shows that the church can be all-encompassing, not just a part or compartment of life, but life itself, all of life, with nothing left out."[35] In its many functions, multiple buildings, and varied architecture, the material culture of Heritage USA embodied the messy integration and easy alliance of religious and secular pursuits that were integral to the Bakkers' worldview. Accounts contemporary to the heyday of Heritage USA and later scholarly reassessments of the Bakkers' headquarters commonly convey the complex, diverse identity of Heritage USA in laundry lists of what it contained: television studio space, worship space, educational buildings, luxury hotels, campgrounds, water park, carousel, skating rink, petting zoo, and tennis courts (see fig. 23).[36] In an attempt to describe the amalgamation of fantasy and recreation, one *Washington Post* reporter described Heritage USA as "somewhere between the Land of Oz and a straight laced Club Med."[37]

Valued at $123 million, Heritage USA was the biggest, most expensive achievement of Jim and Tammy Faye Bakker's 25-year partnership, created with the money their PTL network drew in and ended by Jim Bakker's sexual scandal and financial fraud. Raised in the Pentecostal tradition in Michigan and members of the Assemblies of God Church, Jim (b. 1940) and Tammy Faye (1942–2007) Bakker worked in the 1960s for Pat Robertson's Christian Broadcasting Network in Newport Beach, Virginia, and then for Paul and Jan Crouch's Trinity Broadcasting Network in California, where they began their popular *Praise the Lord* television show. (Notably, Trinity Broadcasting Network owns the Holy Land Experience in

Orlando, Florida, another illustration of the ties between televangelists and theme parks.) In 1974, the Bakkers founded their own PTL television network in Fort Mill, South Carolina. The PTL show and network became the principle means by which the Bakkers gathered money from their "prayer partners" to fund the activities of their religious ministries and the many building projects Jim Bakker dreamed up for Heritage USA. This money also funded their own personal spending. The Bakkers' mansion, a second house in Palm Springs, California, a houseboat, expensive cars including Rolls Royce and Mercedes Benz, an air-conditioned and heated doghouse, and designer clothes and makeup for Tammy Faye signaled an excessive material lifestyle illustrative of the prosperity gospel. In 1987, the Bakkers' PTL empire began to fall. Church secretary Jessica Hahn accused Jim Bakker of rape (a claim Bakker disputed), and Bakker was also accused of engaging in homosexual relationships. These accusations embroiled Jim Bakker in a national sexual scandal featured extensively by Ted Koppel on *Nightline* that undercut Bakker's moralizing messaging and led to his defrocking as a minister of the Assemblies of God Church. In 1988, Bakker was indicted on federal charges of fraud for selling "lifetime memberships" that granted 3-night stays at the 500-room Heritage Grand Hotel at Heritage USA (another hotel at the park, the Heritage Grand Towers, was never completed and today stands as a 21-story ruin), and in 1989 he began serving 5 years of an originally 45-year prison sentence. Jim and Tammy Faye divorced in 1992. In March 1987, following Jim Bakker's resignation from the PTL, Baptist preacher the Reverend Jerry Falwell took over PTL network and Heritage USA. Heritage USA closed two years later in 1989 due to bankruptcy and physical destruction of its buildings and grounds by Hurricane Hugo.[38]

At its zenith in the mid-1980s, Heritage USA was the centerpiece of the Bakkers' PTL network and mission under the umbrella organization of Heritage Village Church. The layout of the grounds of Heritage USA did not put special emphasis on these religious aspects, create specially defined religious zones, or even create a religious center; rather, the more overt religious and missionary functions of the PTL were interwoven throughout the entertainment venues of the park.[39] The half-timbered and gambrel-roofed stone Barn Auditorium (1980) held the Bakkers' worship space and included a later addition of the Broadcast Center (1983) for the PTL network.[40] Also part of this complex was the Total Learning Center, which housed the Heritage Village Church Academy and the School of Evangelism and Communications. Nearby, Bakker created the Upper Room Chapel (1982) as a dedicated small worship space (see fig. 26). The full immersion baptismal pool was located in the Heritage Grand Ministry Center. The World Outreach Center (1981)—a postmodernist, ziggurat-like building with tiered levels encased in dark glass—projected the image of a corporate headquarters visitors saw as they entered the park. Heritage USA was also a place of lived Christian community on the model of evangelical tent revivals. Scattered around the campus were homes for unwed mothers called Heritage House, the homeless in a complex called Fort Hope, and disabled children in a home called Kevin's House.[41] Heritage USA also offered single-family homes, townhouses, apartments, timeshares, hotel rooms, and spaces for recreational vehicles and camping for a variety of length of stays within this Christian community.[42] The Bakkers imagined Heritage USA as a modern update to the tradition of Protestant camp meeting grounds. In a promotional book on Heritage USA, the Bakkers included photographs of "old-fashioned camp meetings" to place Heritage USA within the grand tradition of Protestant camp meetings but also to position it as a way "to carry the spirit of the camp meeting movement into the 21st Century" in "beautiful, pleasant surroundings" with modern conveniences, creating the opposite of "drab, outmoded campgrounds."[43]

The architecture Jim Bakker chose for Heritage USA purposefully allied Christianity with American history, playing on nostalgia for an ideal Christian past. The very name of the park—"Heritage USA"—as the moniker for a Christian theme park invoked civil religion and placed Christianity as the backbone of the American project, drawing on celebrations of America's bicentennial in 1976. As a picture book of Heritage USA proclaimed, "The name 'Heritage USA' expressed a commitment to preserve our Christian and American heritage."[44] To stress the historic connection between Christianity and the founding of the United States, Bakker employed primitive, rustic architecture for large portions of Heritage USA. The log cabin guesthouses at Heritage Village, the wood chalets on Heritage Lake, and rustic wood signage of "Heritage USA" visualized an early American architectural history in a land rich in natural resources, particularly wood. The dedication of the Fort Heritage Campground with a log-cutting ceremony on July 4, 1978, was purposeful symbolism of national patriotism married to Christianity. Fort Heritage and

Buffalo Park within Heritage USA further imagined scenes of America's pioneering past and images of the Old West. This rustic architecture was both celebration of a Christian American history and theme park fodder.[45]

In addition to this rustic early American imagery, Bakker stressed Christianity's significance to the American project by employing Colonial Revival architecture.[46] Before the acquisition of the land in Fort Mill, South Carolina, for Heritage USA, Bakker had developed an earlier, smaller complex in nearby Charlotte, North Carolina, called Heritage Village, the first home of the PTL. The name "Heritage Village" came from a housing development in Michigan where Bakker grew up, and Bakker imagined the Heritage Village complex as something akin to the Colonial Williamsburg theme park in Virginia.[47] Bakker frankly copied elements of Colonial Williamsburg for his Heritage Village, even naming his church and early television studio Bruton Parish Church after the church of the same name in Williamsburg (notwithstanding the fact that the original Bruton Parish Church was Anglican, quite different from Bakker's Pentecostalism).[48] In the building of Heritage USA, Bakker pursued these same Colonial Revival images for their connection to the past and affirmation of good taste. The exterior of the Heritage Grand Hotel, with red brick, white trim, coining, elaborate entablatures, and arched windows, was clearly Colonial Revival, its white colonnade a reference to George Washington's Mount Vernon (fig. 25).[49] In the interior, Chippendale-style furniture (also mixed

with Victorian-style furniture) and multitiered brass chandeliers extended the idea of luxury and the past in the decorative arts. The proposed Heritage Grand Towers was to employ these same elements. The Colonial Revival style also appeared in Heritage USA in appropriated forms. Jim Bakker had the 1927 colonial-style childhood home of evangelist Billy Graham (1918–2018) rebuilt on the grounds of Heritage USA as a purposeful relic of America's Christian past. A glowing account cast Bakker as an ardent preservationist: "Jim Bakker recognizes that our modern 'throw away' society is in danger of losing much of its valuable religious and cultural heritage. . . . Pastor Bakker determined that Heritage Village Church would preserve, promote and bring to life the heritage of our Christian faith and religious roots in America." Although the house was a twentieth-century version of the colonial period, its historical appearance—red brick, white trim, black shutters, simple gable roof, small portico, symmetrical fenestration—visually claimed evangelicalism's long history. Bakker presented Billy Graham's childhood home as "a historic landmark at Heritage USA," another contribution to the landscape of the evangelical theme park.[50]

Much as the rustic and Colonial Revival architecture sought connections to a Christian American heritage, Heritage USA also used architecture to co-locate the authentic birthplace of Christianity to South Carolina. The stone Upper Room Chapel "perfectly recreated" the Upper Room in Jerusalem, the supposed site of the Last Supper and Jesus's appearance to the apostles after his resurrection (fig. 26).[51] The Upper Room Chapel was not simply a worship space but an attempt to place Heritage USA visitors within a re-created experience of the time of Christ and the origins of Christianity to affirm and increase their belief. The re-created Upper Room Chapel was an attempt at the hyperreal, to use Umberto Eco's term, common to theme parks—to make the simulation or copy of the real indistinguishable from the real article itself.[52] Bakker extended this attempt of making Christ's story alive and present to 1980s South Carolina in the construction of the 3,500-seat Jerusalem amphitheater, complete with stage sets depicting the Holy Land, in which the Heritage USA Passion play was performed. Bakker's proposed but never realized Old Jerusalem theme park for Heritage USA, to be built at full scale, would have immersed visitors in the streets of Old Jerusalem in another approximation of Christ's story, though this time in South Carolina and this time in the late twentieth century. Bakker hoped that the Old Jerusalem re-creation would "awaken a greater understanding of historic Christian heritage" as another component within the evangelical theme park.[53]

The sum effect of Jim Bakker's multiple architectural styles—rustic, colonial, Middle Eastern, and Victorian (Bakker had also planned Farmland USA, a village in the Victorian style, for Heritage USA)—was to create a theme park of an imagined Christian past, one rooted in images of the Holy Land and of a storied American

history for which Christianity was the founding myth. Just as Disneyland and Disney World used multiple architectural styles to create a world set apart (think here of the juxtaposition of Victorian-style Main Street to the German-influenced castle at Disney World, or the architecture of Japan juxtaposed immediately next to the architecture of Morocco at EPCOT), Bakker easily and without contradiction put multiple architectural styles in conversation. Heritage USA was clearly a theme park whose theme centered on a Christian past. As a 1990 long-form article on the Bakkers in the *New Yorker* saw it, "Heritage USA was a parody of postmodern architecture, theme parks, historical reconstruction, and perhaps popular culture as a whole."[54]

At Heritage USA, just as at Disney, alongside the nostalgia for an imagined past was a frank focus on entertainment and recreation. Scattered throughout the park were opportunities for fun: a carousel, miniature train, a petting zoo, roller-skating rink, tennis courts, and multiple swimming pools. The centerpiece of Heritage USA's entertainment programming was the Heritage Island water park, completed in 1986 at the center of the park. Heritage Island included a lazy river, a wave pool, and "The Typhoon" double waterslide that promised a thrilling 35-mile-per-hour drop (fig. 27). As a promotional book described, "Heritage Island inspirational water park provides, fun, recreation, live Christian music, refreshments and fellowship in a wholesome family atmosphere."[55] This focus on Christian music, fellowship, and a wholesome family atmosphere sanctified the leisure time of Heritage USA visitors. Heritage USA's message was clear: the Christian lifestyle could be carried out at all times, in all aspects of life.

Those wanting a less physical form of recreation found it in the Main Street shopping mall located between the Heritage Grand Hotel and the Ministry Center on the shores of Heritage Lake. This interior space—covered with a curved roof painted in blue to mimic the sky and lit with an ethereal light—was an unabashed version of Disney's Main Street, USA in its Victorian-style storefronts in pastel

**Figure 27.** View of the Heritage Island water park at Heritage USA from the top of the Typhoon waterslide in a 2006 photograph. Note the exteriors (at center top, from left to right) of the Heritage Grand Hotel, Main Street, and Heritage Grand Ministry Center. (Photograph by Robin Nelson/ZUMA Press, Inc./Alamy Stock Photo; © Copyright 2006 by Robin Nelson)

**Figure 28.** Main Street at Heritage USA. (Photograph by Margaret M. Grubiak)

colors (fig. 28). The shopping and services here included tongue-in-cheek references to religion and the past framed within American consumer culture. Visitors could buy candy at the Heavenly Fudge Shoppe, the Susie Moppet Doll that played a recording of Tammy Faye's voice at Noah's Toy Shoppe, souvenir trinkets from Heritage Gift Shoppe, and books on faith and salvation from Ye Olde Bookstore. Just like Tammy Faye—famous for her designer wardrobe and heavy makeup, especially her thick, black mascara which would frequently run down her face with her tears during her PTL testimonials—women could indulge in ways to enhance their external appearance, buying Tammy Faye–endorsed cosmetics, having their hair done at the Royal Hair Design, and purchasing jewelry. The Main Street shopping mall even sold lingerie in support of healthy marriages.[56] In a 1989 study of consumerism at Heritage USA, Thomas O'Guinn and Russell Belk argued "at Heritage Village the consumption of religious and secular offerings has been forged into a single ethos in which both are sacred rites. Not only has religion become a consumption object, consumption has become a religion in which wealth and opulence are venerated."[57] When understood within the ideals of the prosperity gospel, this comingling of religion and consumption at Heritage USA was not surprising at all.

A site of religious devotion, recreation, consumption, and television production, Heritage USA mirrored the theme park as codified by Disney while innovating the subgenre of the evangelical theme park. Heritage USA was lavish, and it was supposed to be. Roe Messner, head of construction for Heritage USA and later second husband of Tammy Faye, called Heritage USA "the eighth wonder of the world."[58] But the downfall of Jim Bakker in scandal and imprisonment cast another light on Heritage USA. Heritage USA is now a ruin. The never-completed twenty-one-story Heritage Grand Towers, surrounded by chain-link fencing, is marred with broken windows. Some of its brick cladding has fallen to the ground. Townhomes now occupy Heritage Island, with all signs of the water park removed. While MorningStar Ministries currently operates out of the Heritage Grand Hotel, Main Street still stands, and the Upper Room Chapel remains open to visitors, gone is any cohesive sense of Heritage USA as an evangelical theme park. Heritage USA as a ruin symbolizes Bakker's hubris and the excesses of American televangelism. At its height in the 1980s, Heritage USA was a vibrant landscape of Pentecostal faith, but now in its ruin we read it as a failure of that faith, or at least the Bakkers' lavish, expensive, and entertaining version of it.

## Falwell's Plunge

The Heritage Island water park at Heritage USA was the centerpiece of a famous satiric image generated not by outside detractors but by the very man who took over the Praise the Lord network and Heritage USA after Jim Bakker's fall: the Reverend Jerry Falwell. Falwell (1933–2007), a Southern Baptist preacher, founder of Liberty University in Lynchburg, Virginia, and the conservative political group the Moral Majority, and televangelist with his own *The Old-Time Gospel Hour* show, assumed leadership of the PTL after a contentious battle in March 1987.[59] In an effort to raise much-needed funds to keep Heritage USA open, Falwell promised that he and fellow PTL presenter Doug Oldham would go down Heritage Island's 60-foot-high

Typhoon waterslide on television when the one thousandth financial pledge was made to the PTL "Resurrection Committee." The fundraising stunt was successful, drawing in $22 million, and on September 10, 1987, Falwell went down the slide as promised. The event was broadcast live on *The PTL Club* program. To maximize publicity, national press outlets including the Associated Press and United Press International newswires were invited to record Falwell's stunt.[60] Photographer Andy Burriss captured a black-and-white, tightly cropped photograph of Falwell dressed in full suit midslide for the Associated Press, an image that was broadcast around the world in publications such as the *Chicago Tribune* and *Time* (fig. 29).[61] The image became so iconic that the Associated Press named it among its top one hundred photographs of the twentieth century. This photograph, as well as the televised broadcast, generated a satiric image of Heritage USA as framed by Falwell himself, who compared the cartoonish image of his fall down a waterslide to the image of Pope John Paul II's dignified arrival in Miami that very same day. Falwell's own self-conscious comments

**Figure 29.** The Reverend Jerry Falwell descending the Typhoon waterslide at Heritage USA, September 10, 1987. (AP Photo/The Herald, Andy Burriss)

raised questions over the relationship of entertainment, money, and religion. While for Jim and Tammy Faye Bakker and other believers in the prosperity gospel these categories had easy overlap, Jerry Falwell embodied contrary views about the proper role and dignity of religion in the public sphere.

A series of contrasts focused on Jerry Falwell's own body generated the humor and ultimate satire of his plunge down the waterslide. Falwell's Halston designer navy suit, button-down white dress shirt, undershirt, suspenders, red tie, and dark socks (he removed his dress shoes to go down the slide) were at odds with the informal setting of the water park and entirely nonfunctional for his immersion into water. The incongruence of his attire was made more prominent as the camera showed him climbing up the slide's staircase as female lifeguards, dressed in more appropriate but much more revealing swimsuits, lined the walkway. As a joke at Falwell's expense, fellow PTL presenter Doug Oldham slapped a sticker reading "Farewell Falwell" on his back. The audience's laughter came not just at the message itself but also at the knowledge of its double-coded meaning: the bumper sticker was originally made by backers of Jim Bakker during the fight over control of the PTL, which Falwell had won.[62] Adding to the absurdity of the situation, at the top of the slide behind the suit-clad Falwell was a person dressed in an "Allie the Alligator" costume complete with a lifeguard T-shirt. For those watching, these dissonant images provoked laughter—an audience-generated laugh track to accompany the televised images—just as they were intended to do.

Falwell and his PTL companions framed his fate, tongue-in-cheek, in Christological themes of death, rebirth, and belief immediately recognized by the news reports of the event. In banter before the plunge, Falwell focused on the possibility of his own death. He half-jokingly recited the Lord's Prayer and part of Psalm 23: "The Lord is my shepherd; I shall not want. He maketh me to lie down in green pastures. He leadeth me beside the still waters."[63] Recalling the image of Christ as the sacrificial lamb who willingly accepted his fate, he said, "Like a lamb led to the slaughter, we'll open not our mouths."[64] The slide was renamed in the PTL broadcast from "The Typhoon" to the more ominous "The Killer Typhoon," and as Falwell joked about surviving death, the camera panned to an ambulance standing nearby in case something should go awry. As he lay down on the waterslide, Falwell recited, "Now I lay me down to sleep. I pray the Lord my soul to keep."[65]

When Falwell finally did go down the slide after much anticipation, his body seemed to fulfill this possibility of death but also the possibility of rebirth. The iconic photograph of Falwell's descent midslide captured his body in a posture the Associated Press and others called "corpse-like"—lying on his back, his arms crossed over his chest, eyes closed.[66] Yet when we consider Falwell's identity as a Christian, Baptist leader, his chairmanship of the PTL, and the setting of a Christian space (even if a Christian theme park), Falwell's corpse-like body in that moment became something more: an approximation of a sacrificial Jesus Christ, only not at Golgotha but at a water park. And just as Jesus would rise from his bodily death, Falwell's safe arrival in the splash pool below also invoked rebirth, not only in the

**Figure 30.** The Reverend Jerry Falwell emerging from the water after his descent on the Typhoon. (Photograph by Robin Nelson/ZUMA Press, Inc./Alamy Stock Photo; © Copyright by Robin Nelson)

sense of baptism in water (fitting for a Baptist preacher) but also in the sense of Christ's resurrection, an idea inherent in the "Resurrection Committee" name in which the pledges to the PTL were made (fig. 30). Even the double entendre of Falwell's own name—to fall, well—played into the idea of those chosen for salvation and the safety within the belief in Christ. One final gag revealed a larger truth: although Doug Oldham had pledged that he would also go down the slide, the jokester Oldham instead sent down a dummy dressed in a suit, presumably to escape any danger or death. Yet the contrast between the inanimate dummy and the very animate Falwell in the splash pool below cast these figures in the roles of nonbeliever and believer, with Falwell's "survival" of the fall proof of what faith in God and Christ can mean. Although in an exaggerated way, the slide down the Typhoon was not mere theme park entertainment but a reenactment of the Passion of Christ—a different kind of theater than the Passion play performed elsewhere at the park.

Falwell's personal risk in the face of bodily harm appeared to be his sacrifice for the greater good of the Heritage USA organization and its attendant evangelical mission. Yet as framed by Falwell himself, his sacrifice was actually of the seriousness of religion for the unseriousness of entertainment. This self-conscious interpretation hinged on the happenstance of Pope John Paul II's arrival in Miami for an official visit to the United States on the very same day as Falwell's plunge. Video footage captured the moment Falwell walked out of the pool after the plunge, holding a microphone given to him by an aide, and toward the media scrum and audience that had just witnessed his plummet down the slide. As he arose from the water to the awaiting press conference, he asked, "Do we really have to do this?" signaling his embarrassment and discomfort and setting up the importance of the contrast Falwell himself then made to the awaiting audience: "Can you imagine the fun on split screen television news tonight with a distinguished pope stepping off of a plane from Rome in Miami and this nut, this Baptist preacher coming down a waterslide for $22 million little dollars?"[67] In this comment, Falwell generated his own satiric image, again based on contrast: the "distinguished Pope" descending steps from his plane dressed in his white papal robes met by President Ronald Reagan and First Lady Nancy Reagan for an official state visit while "this nut, this Baptist preacher" emerged from the water dripping wet in his dark suit to meet a press scrum gathered for a publicity and fundraising stunt. The pope's purpose was for serious and dignified pastoral work. As Pope John Paul II said in remarks on the Miami airport tarmac, "I come as a pilgrim, a pilgrim in the cause of justice and peace and human solidarity, striving to build up the one human family."[68] Falwell's purpose, on the other hand, was to gather, in his own words, "little dollars" and to create a publicity spectacle.[69] The cartoonish aspect of the stunt was underscored by the PTL itself. Immediately after Falwell's descent, *The PTL Club* played back the footage of his free fall, adding the sound effect of the slide whistle often used in animated cartoons.[70] Falwell's spokesman said the stunt "was the first hour of levity we've had" since the PTL's June 1987 bankruptcy declaration over the Bakker scandal.[71]

While we might read Jerry Falwell's remarks as self-deprecating humor, Falwell's comments confirmed his self-consciousness of the image of dignity and gravity upheld by the pope and the opposite image he himself had just created. A *New York Times* piece noted the contrast of the two images, stating that "there was nothing particularly unbecoming about" Falwell's stunt but arguing that the pope would never do the same since "part of [the pope's] charisma is his gravity."[72] It was this gravity that Falwell was so highly conscious of due to his fundamentalist Baptist beliefs. For Falwell, religion was serious business. In her study of Jerry Falwell, anthropologist Susan Friend Harding writes, "Jerry Falwell, his empire, and his allies stood for production, hard work, restraint, sacrifice, delayed gratification, steady growth, contained crises, hierarchy, male dominance, sexual repression, obedience to Godly others, the Word, narrative structure and authority, fixed identity, place, authenticity, depth, and centeredness."[73] Harding argues that Jim and Tammy Faye Bakker were precisely the opposite and that they used Christian fundamentalism as the "cultural other" by which to hone their own Pentecostal identity. So while Falwell and his Baptist fundamentalism was concerned about "restraint" and "authenticity," Jim and Tammy Faye in their Pentecostalism reveled in "spectacle" and "artifice."[74] While Falwell was no stranger to begging for money—he raised more than $1 million per week through both written and televised appeals by the early 1980s—he did not typically do so in performances like the waterslide stunt.[75] Falwell's own *The Old-Time Gospel Hour* television shows were staid by comparison. As Harding argues, "Ignoring television's built-in preference for visually dramatic performances, Falwell seemed to be all story and no spectacle."[76] The Bakkers, by contrast, built the PTL on spectacle. Had Jim Bakker been the one to go down the slide for the $22 million, he would have relished it. But for Jerry Falwell, a Baptist from a different religious conviction and a more stiff and serious disposition, the spectacle of going down the slide was discomfiting. That Falwell had once declared that there would be "no more sideshows" on the Praise the Lord network suggests his apparent discomfort with the waterslide sideshow was real.[77]

Jerry Falwell's self-consciousness of how his descent down the waterslide would play in public vis-à-vis the pope's visit transformed the meaning of the event. Falwell's incompatibility with the PTL and its Pentecostal culture proved to be too much. Citing the sheer scale of the PTL and Heritage USA's financial debts, Falwell resigned from the PTL on October 8, 1987, just twenty-eight days after his plunge down the slide.[78] The black-and-white, tightly cropped Associated Press photograph of Falwell descending the slide captured in one image the tension between religion and money, Pentecostal and fundamentalist Protestantism, and a vision of religion as possessing gravity and dignity and a vision of religion as joyful and lighthearted.

### Heritage USA as Praiseland: *The Simpsons'* Satire of Pentecostal Belief

If the image of Jerry Falwell's plunge brought into sharp focus the dissonance of religion and entertainment for some, then another response to Heritage USA by *The Simpsons* satirized more directly Pentecostal theology and religious belief writ large. In the 2001 episode "I'm Goin' to Praiseland," Springfield's resident evangelical Ned Flanders constructed a Christian theme park in honor of his dead wife Maude. (Given that the copyright holder of *The Simpsons,* Twentieth Century Fox Film Corporation, did not grant permission to publish an image of Praiseland in this book, readers are encouraged to seek out the image readily available online.)

The episode's writers specifically noted in a commentary on the episode that they based Praiseland on Heritage USA, though Heritage USA had closed eleven years earlier.[79] Like Heritage USA, Praiseland was imagined as a theme park for good, clean Christian fun. As Ned said, "We're going to show Springfield that faith and devotion are the wildest thrill rides of all!"[80] The cartoonists drew the greatest hits of Christianity for Praiseland: a Tree of Knowledge from the Garden of Eden, complete with apples and snake; a Temple of Solomon; the Tower of Babel; Noah's Ark; a nativity; and Golgotha on a hill with three crosses. Much as Heritage USA sought to bring biblical times to life in its proposed re-creation of the Holy Land and performances of the Passion play, the fictional Praiseland became an experiential Bible infused with religious-themed fun and games.

Yet *The Simpsons* drew laughs by undermining the idea that religion could actually be fun. "King David's Wild Ride" was more metaphorical rather than literal: Bart Simpson and his friends found their roller-coaster ride stopped short by a towering and menacing King David animatronic figure who wanted to read them all of his psalms. The park included games such as "Whack-A-Satan," a play on the carnival game "Whack-A-Mole," but offered no bat to whack the pop-up Satans since Ned believed you could get them with faith alone.[81] The souvenir of a miniature Noah's Ark filled with candy jellies failed to entice too. Such games and rides did not live up to the expectation of an "amusement" park to the residents of fictional Springfield. As the character Sideshow Mel proclaimed, "This place is the height of tedium!"[82] To these non-evangelicals, a religious theme park was a contradiction in terms.

After undermining the idea of the evangelical theme park, episode writer Julie Thacker crafted a satire of Pentecostal belief. Just as the Springfield residents began to leave Praiseland, a miracle seemed to happen that put the focus on religious faith rather than religious fun. A mask of Maude's face floated up to her memorial statue at the center of the park, leading people to believe that Maude's statue had miraculous powers. Suddenly Principal Skinner fell in front of the statue, started speaking in tongues, and gave witness to a vision of heaven, playing on Pentecostal beliefs of speaking in tongues and having visions. Others also began to experience visions of heaven as they stood or knelt before the statue, and Maude's statue was transformed into a religious shrine and a place for miracles. But soon Homer and Ned discover that a gas leak caused the floating Maude head and the hallucinations of the Spring-field residents, a storyline that had its roots in a real gas leak on opening day at Disneyland in California in 1955. What seemed to be a miracle—a real connection with the divine—had a rational explanation.

In two acts, the writer of this *Simpsons* episode negated the two underlying premises of the evangelical theme park: first, that it is possible to combine religion and fun; and second, that religious belief is true. Undermining the belief of Pentecostal theology was a particularly biting satire in this episode. As David Edwin Harrell Jr. recounts in his study of postwar charismatic revival, Pentecostals believe in "continual personal encounters with God." Pentecostals have a particular belief in the supernatural as evidence of the Holy Spirit. The Holy Spirit is central to their baptism and also confers nine spiritual gifts, among which are speaking in tongues, prophecy, healing, and miracles.[83] This profound belief in the supernatural, evidenced in outward displays such as speaking in tongues, was easy for *The Simpsons* writer to undermine. What the residents of Springfield believed to be a miracle turned out not to be. Their speaking in tongues and hallucinations of heaven could be explained with a scientific, physical cause. Moreover, that Bart and Homer Simpson raised the entrance fee to the park once the public became aware of the apparent miracles played on the idea of Pentecostal televangelists' exploitation of their followers, drawing a straight line to Jim Bakker. While the plotline of *The Simpsons* episode did not follow the financial and sexual scandals of the PTL and Jim Bakker that mesmerized the nation, Jim Bakker similarly enacted a fraud in taking advantage of people's faith for his own material gain. Just as Praiseland was shuttered (because Ned and Homer tackled children to prevent the lighting of devotional candles, which could have set off a gas explosion), Heritage USA was also shuttered in what could be understood as justice for exploiting people's desire for religious affirmation and connection.

Both reframings of Heritage USA captured in the photograph of Jerry Falwell's plunge and in *The Simpsons*' Praiseland episode foregrounded questions about religion's relationship to entertainment and money as well as core elements of Pentecostal theology. For Falwell, his public humiliation on Heritage USA's waterslide called into question the public display of religion as entertainment that was at odds with the conception of religion as dignified and serious as it confronts the most important questions and struggles of life. *The Simpsons,* a popular culture critique, went beyond Falwell's self-caricature in drawing out the possibilities and implications of hollow belief. Both responses operate in anxieties about how we express religion materially in our world; how we acknowledge religious belief in our daily lives, including our recreation time; the entire enterprise of televangelism, which seeks to follow Christ's commandment to spread the Gospel around the world but comes into conflict with profane issues such as money and corrupting power; and even the substance of what we believe.

## Oral Roberts University: A Religious World's Fair

Just as Heritage USA housed Jim and Tammy Faye Bakker's Praise the Lord network and ministries, Oral Roberts University in Tulsa, Oklahoma, served as the headquarters for the ministries and production of radio and television shows of Pentecostal-turned-Methodist televangelist Oral Roberts (fig. 31).[84] After decades as

**Figure 31.** Oral Roberts University in Tulsa, Oklahoma, with Prayer Tower (center) and John D. Messick Learning Resources Center (left), ca. 1960s. (Beryl Ford Collection/Rotary Club of Tulsa, Tulsa City-County Library and Tulsa Historical Society, Tulsa, Oklahoma)

an itinerant tent revival preacher, Granville Oral Roberts (1918–2009) founded his eponymous university in 1963 and opened it in 1965 to establish a physical home for his many ministries and to confer upon himself the respectability that came with a nationally accredited university. Alongside his architect Frank Wallace, Oral Roberts crafted a campus in a futuristic and opulent architectural imagery that simultaneously spoke to middle-class luxury, the Space Age, and the electronic church. Among the extraordinary buildings on the Oral Roberts University campus, two in particular stand out: the 200-foot mirrored Prayer Tower, crafted as an abstracted cross of Christ modeled after the Seattle Space Needle, and the City of Faith, a trio of skyscrapers for a hospital, medical clinic, and medical school that carried out Roberts's lifelong Pentecostal belief in healing through prayer. The Prayer Tower and City of Faith became the objects of religious satire as Roberts claimed visions of a 900-foot Jesus and God threatening his life if he failed to raise money for his ministries. Like the reframings of Heritage USA, the satire of Oral Roberts University trained its skepticism on Pentecostal theology and the role of money within American televangelism.

Oral Roberts University is more than a university—it is an evangelical theme park informed by the architecture of the Disney parks and world's fairs. Oral Roberts crafted his campus as his own version of a world's fair and amusement park and fairgrounds with an explicit religious message. As we have already seen, the futuristic Space Age architecture of Oral Roberts University recalls Tomorrowland (opened in 1955) at Disneyland, while the colorful Prayer Tower offers rides to an observation deck much like the Space Needle from the 1962 Seattle World's Fair and Philip Johnson's New York State Pavilion for the 1964–65 New York World's Fair. The "Avenue of Flags" at the campus entrance showcasing the countries of Oral Roberts University students added to the sense of a fair, further increased by the addition of a giant, 60-foot-tall *Healing Hands* sculpture originally commissioned for the City of Faith complex in 1980 and moved to the campus entrance ten years later. The carefully ordered grounds of the campus—the lavish sunken gardens, the inscribed geometries, and the architecturally unified buildings radiating out from the centralized Prayer Tower—read not just as a university campus but also as fairgrounds. (Not coincidentally, Tulsa is also home to the annual Tulsa State Fair, which first opened in 1961, one of two state fairs in Oklahoma, located less than ten miles from Oral

Roberts University.) These allusions to fairgrounds and amusement parks prompted the description of the campus as "Six Flags Over Jesus," a reference to the Six Flags Over Texas theme park, which opened in 1961 just outside of Dallas, in addition to an "educational and spiritual Disneyland."[85] The complexity of the campus of Oral Roberts University, much like the complexity of Heritage USA, is that it is many things at once—a university, production studios, Oral Roberts's headquarters, and a religious world's fair—that came to define the evangelical theme park.

One world's fair in particular—the 1962 Seattle World's Fair—had an outsized influence on the design of the Oral Roberts University campus. In May 1963, less than seven months after the fair closed, Oral Roberts conducted a crusade on the Seattle fairgrounds.[86] During this visit, Roberts would have seen the Seattle Space Needle and walked around the grounds, perhaps visiting the U.S. Science Pavilion science exhibition buildings (now called the Pacific Science Center) designed by architect Minoru Yamasaki.[87] Roberts was immersed in this environment just as he was thinking through the plans for his own university then under construction.[88] The influence of the Seattle fair on the Oral Roberts University campus was clear. A *Progressive Architecture* article—referencing architects Minoru Yamasaki and Oscar Niemeyer, designer of Brazil's capital Brasilia from the 1950s—described the Oral Roberts University campus "looking as if it crystallizes the dream of a Yamasaki designing Brasilia after he had seen the Seattle World's Fair."[89]

Oral Roberts's co-opting of the architecture of the Seattle fair, known officially as the Century 21 Exposition, for his own campus was intentional. In doing so, Roberts signaled the same themes as the Seattle fair: Christianity's centrality to the future and to the fight over good and evil manifested in the Cold War. Planning for the Seattle fair was underway when the Russians launched the Sputnik satellite in 1957, ushering in the space race within the Cold War. American evangelists framed religion as a critical partner in the Cold War. Evangelist Billy Graham, as historian Andrew Preston has claimed, "explicitly linked the cause of Christ with the cause of America, of Christianity's struggle against Satan with America's struggle against communism."[90] This Christian struggle was also linked directly to America's space race efforts. The architecture of the fair, particularly Minoru Yamasaki's U.S. Science Pavilion, imaged this comingling of science and religion with five white, freestanding towers formed from pointed, "space Gothic" arches positioned in the

**Figure 32.** View of the Century 21 Exposition, Seattle, Washington, 1962, with the United States Science Pavilion by architect Minoru Yamasaki (*center*) and the Christian Witness Pavilion (*right*). (Photograph by Max R. Jensen published by C. P. Johnston Co., postcard in the personal collection of Margaret M. Grubiak)

middle of the pavilion (fig. 32). This religious imagery was understood by fairgoers, including one critic who described Yamasaki's buildings as possessing a "religious" character.[91] Religion was also explicitly present at the fair in three pavilions devoted to various religious denominations, including the Christian Witness Pavilion whose location immediately next to the U.S. Science Pavilion signaled religion's important role to craft meaning among technology and to counter godless communism with a Christian-focused democracy (see fig. 32). These themes would have been inescapable to Oral Roberts as he toured the grounds, and these themes would be repeated in the architecture of Oral Roberts University that reified the electronic church within a permanent religious world's fair.[92]

Two key buildings at the Seattle fair—Yamasaki's U.S. Science Pavilion and the iconic Space Needle—became touchstones for the vision of Oral Roberts University's architecture. The style of Yamasaki's buildings known as New Formalism— a restrained use of classicism that included elegant colonnades; a renewed use of ornament, particularly in brise soleil; and a color palette of white, black, and gold— moved outside the strictures of postwar modernism to craft an image of elegance and wealth. Oral Roberts seized on New Formalism to appeal to students from a mostly white, Protestant middle class.[93] Echoing the critical reception of the 1974 Mormon Washington D.C. Temple, another New Formalist building criticized for its popular culture references (see chapter 2), a 1978 assessment published in *Progressive Architecture* claimed that Oral Roberts University represented "a kind of popular understanding of modern architecture" tinged with an idea of luxury:

> The aesthetic reflects that of a new middle class whose aspirations are toward elegance—an elegance that is somewhat standardized and perhaps a bit gaudy to ensure that the point not be missed. It is designed to be impressive, in other words. Yet the impressiveness is as comfortably predictable as one would expect in a good motel; it is slightly overpriced "Ramada-mentality."[94]

As Thomas Hine has termed it, this "populuxe," or popular luxury, image was an assertion of good taste and "symbols of achievement, affirmations that their owners had achieved a life of convenience and prosperity that their parents could have only dreamed of."[95] Most of the buildings at Oral Roberts University aligned with this New Formalist language in a remarkable architecturally cohesive campus.

If Yamasaki's aesthetic informed the New Formalist architectural language for much of the Oral Roberts University campus, then the Space Needle for the Seattle Fair was the blueprint for Oral Roberts's iconic structure, the Prayer Tower, which Roberts called "the logo for the university" (fig. 33).[96] The final design of the Prayer Tower, constructed in 1967, directly referenced the Seattle Space Needle.[97] For the Seattle fair, architect John Graham Jr. and businessman Edward E. Carlson imagined a 605-foot structure elegant in shape: a tripod-like supporting structure

pinched near the top supporting a gleaming round saucer holding a rotating restaurant (fig. 34).[98] For the Oral Roberts University campus, architect Frank Wallace created a Prayer Tower that trafficked in the same futuristic language as the Space Needle, a similarity clearly recognized in press descriptions of the Prayer Tower as "a space needle."[99] Although a third of the height of the Space Needle at 200 feet and with a different supporting structure, the Prayer Tower also showcased a saucer-like observation level that compared closely to the Space Needle. Like the Space Needle's metallic cladding, the Prayer Tower's mirrored gold, blue, and white surfaces gleam in the sun.

The Prayer Tower reminded students, visitors, and Roberts's television audience alike "that prayer and the power of God are central to all we do" within Oral Roberts's ministry and the university.[100] From afar, the tower's form looked like a cross. Up close, those looking up at the tower saw a symmetrical web of steel that was to recall Jesus's crown of thorns. To stress this analogy, the tips of steel in the crown were colored red to symbolize the blood of Christ. From above, this crown of thorns also appeared as the Star of David. At the very top of the tower was an eternal flame, representing the Holy Spirit. The Prayer Tower asserted Christ in the daily experience of the campus and visualized the mission of Roberts's ministry explicitly. The Prayer Tower at Oral Roberts University is an unusual building in the history of campus design.[101] Drawing on the form of the Seattle Space Needle and overlaying a religious function and iconography, the Prayer Tower helped craft the image of Oral Roberts University as a religious world's fair.

The futuristic and opulent architectural image of Oral Roberts University created a new architectural language for the electronic church in America. More than a university, the campus was a stage set, appearing in Roberts's *Contact* television specials. Its opulent and futuristic image helped convey Roberts's health and wealth gospel and visualize religion's relevance to the modern age. But the fantastic architecture of the campus also became the locus of satire of Roberts's religious belief, transforming the campus from a landscape of belief into a landscape of doubt. The Prayer Tower and the City of Faith became stage sets in other ways, this time for a critique of Oral Roberts, his beliefs, and his ministry.

**Figure 34.** Space Needle at the 1962 Seattle World's Fair, Century 21 Exposition, John Graham Jr. and Edward E. Carlson, Seattle, Washington. (University of Washington Libraries, Special Collections, UW29989z)

## A 900-Foot Jesus in the City of Faith and a "Death Watch" in the Prayer Tower

Oral Roberts's profound and lifelong belief in the healing power of faith — a core tenet of Pentecostalism — led him to build the enormous, and enormously expensive, City of Faith. A later addition to the Oral Roberts University campus, the City of Faith included a medical school, hospital, and medical clinic. While Roberts had long wanted to build a medical school for his university, the tragic death of his daughter and son-in-law in a plane crash in 1977 led him to a time of reflection in the Palm Springs, California, desert during which he claimed to have a vision for the complex. Roberts said God inspired the name "City of Faith" based on the City of God—the New Jerusalem—described in the Book of Revelation.[102] To stress this biblical connection, the City of Faith grounds included a 40-foot-wide stream lined with evergreen trees to represent the River of Life and the Tree of Life in the City of God as foretold in the Book of Revelation. The architectural form for the City of Faith came to Roberts in his vision: a 60-story medical clinic tower, a 30-story hospital, and a 20-story research tower (fig. 35). Architect Frank Wallace brought Roberts's vision to life in skyscrapers framed in the familiar Oral Roberts University gold, white, and black color palette. The same language of New Formalist architecture on the rest of the campus was on full display in this complex as well, with the angularity of the International Style box tempered with the addition of dynamic polygonal and triangular shapes in mirrored gold glass, inscribed with crosses patterned after the Prayer Tower. Roberts imagined the City of Faith as "a great national and world center of medicine and prayer" where faith healing would

**Figure 35.** City of Faith (now CityPlex Towers), Oral Roberts University, architect Frank Wallace, Tulsa, Oklahoma, 1978–81. (Photograph by Storer, published by Storer's Cards, Inc., postcard in the personal collection of Margaret M. Grubiak)

occur alongside modern medicine.[103] While the construction of the complex led to a heated battle over the need to add a massive hospital to Tulsa, a battle eventually resolved in the Oklahoma Supreme Court, the complex opened in 1981.[104] Roberts commissioned sculptor Leonard D. McMurry to create an enormous 60-foot sculpture of hands grasped in prayer symbolizing "the hand of prayer and the hand of medicine joined together" at the base of the towers (see fig. 22).[105] The City of Faith and the Prayer Tower were the most visible symbols of Roberts's belief in faith healing, and they became a lightning rod for criticism when that belief intermingled with claims of religious visions for money and for Roberts's life.

As discussed in the introduction, Roberts's extraordinary claim in 1980 of a vision a 900-foot tall Jesus appearing to him in support of the City of Faith drew satirical responses that visualized a landscape of doubt. In a September 1980 appeal for money to fund the $120 million City of Faith, Roberts told his prayer partners that Jesus said, "I would speak to your partners and through them I WOULD BUILD IT."[106] Roberts's claim spurred a backlash of doubt and derision at the idea of a 900-foot Jesus appearing on Earth. As we have seen, among the most biting responses was a photograph with the City of Faith buildings in the background with a doctored sign that read "BEGIN 900 FT. JESUS X-ING" and included an image of Jesus in silhouette (see fig. 1). A poster of the photograph professionalized and commercialized the satire for profit. The poster gained a wider audience when the Associated Press circulated a reproduction of it, which ran in the *Saturday Oklahoman and Times* newspaper in 1981.[107] The creation of the poster was a local act, but the publication of the poster in newspapers made the satire more widely available.

The photograph's juxtaposition of the altered sign with the City of Faith buildings is a powerful visual religious satire. This photograph made visible Roberts's claim, putting it in context within the physical landscape of the Oral Roberts University and the City of Faith. The centerpiece of the satire is the altered road sign. The sign appears to be official, co-opting government-issued road signs warning drivers of railroad crossings or animal crossings through the wording of "BEGIN" and "X-ING." The sign seems to give Roberts's vision official sanction and therefore credibility. The inclusion of the word "BEGIN" importantly assigns ownership of the vision to Oral Roberts by locating it within the boundaries of his campus. At the same time, the sign also confers ownership of the extraordinary vision to all who read it (via the poster), making the audience an involuntary participant in and witness to the vision. The sign also makes Roberts's vision permanent: the vision was not just something that Roberts had on May 25, 1980, at 7:00 p.m., as he claimed, but it is a vision that is renewed each time someone reads the sign via the poster. The sign further suggests Jesus's continued presence in the area and that Jesus might be glimpsed at any moment. The 900-foot Jesus was no longer something privately experienced by Oral Roberts but rather something publicly witnessed again and again by those who, through their own physical vision and reading, became part of the vision and also part of the satire of it.

As we read the text of the sign, we also see and understand its central image: a graphic of Jesus. Between "900 FT." at the top of the sign and "JESUS X-ING" at the bottom of the sign is an image of Jesus in black silhouette, just as another road sign might include a graphic of a deer or other animal. We know it is Jesus through recognizable clues drawing on visualizations of Jesus in the popular imagination. We can discern Jesus's beard and his long, tiered robes. We see him in the posture of prayer, with his head tilted upward toward heaven and his hands grasped in prayer. This prayerful posture echoes the silhouette of the real *Healing Hands* statue then located at the entrance to the City of Faith we simultaneously see in the background of the photograph. Here, the graphic and statue reinforce each other. While the scale of the graphic of Jesus on the sign alone seems small, the words "900 FT." above the image instruct us to imagine the scale as enormous. This large scale is further emphasized in the photograph itself, where the Jesus graphic in the foreground and the towering skyscrapers in the background appear to be in closer parity as the small trees in the middle ground seem to shrink in comparison. Here, text and image work together to underscore the scale of Roberts's vision of Jesus, which was at the core of the satires and skepticism of it.

The altered sign within the photograph of the City of Faith has great power as a religious satire because it puts Roberts's vision in the context of the real, situating an image of a 900-foot Jesus in the actual landscape of Oral Roberts University. The satire is embedded in the sign itself—the words mock the idea of a 900-foot Jesus and that Jesus (a giant one) could be routinely seen in the area—but the altered photograph frames the City of Faith itself as an object of satirical response. The paradox is that Roberts's vision, at least in part, was realized: he raised enough money that the City of Faith was completed. The doctored sign nevertheless pushed back against Roberts's claim, vocalizing a reaction against taking advantage of people's religious faith for money and doubt over the Pentecostal belief in religious visions.

Seven years after Oral Roberts's vision of a 900-foot Jesus, Roberts made a second extraordinary claim in January 1987: God told Roberts that he would "call me home" if Roberts did not raise $4.5 million (later raised to $8 million) to fund a medical missionary program by the following March.[108] Roberts wrote to his partners that "God said, 'I want you to use the ORU medical school to put My medical presence in the earth. I want you to get this going in one year or I will call you home!'" He appealed to them: "I desperately need you to come into agreement with me concerning my life being extended beyond March."[109] Roberts faced immediate backlash with critics calling his plea emotional blackmail. How much was Roberts's life worth? How much might God, who supposedly was going to render judgment in the form of a death sentence, value a human life in terms of human economy and dollars? Garry Trudeau's popular *Doonesbury* comic played on these questions in what became one of the most visible satires of Roberts's threat. Trudeau ran a series of cartoons in February 1987 that called the event "God's extraordinary $4.5 million shakedown."[110] *Doonesbury* imagined conversations about the validity of Roberts's claim between an unbelieving son and believing mother and between radio personalities as they broadcast the "Oral Roberts Death Watch" call-in show. One cartoon wondered if God put a $4.5 million bounty on Roberts's life, then how much might God ask for the life of Woody Allen, Jerry Garcia, or Vanna White (fig. 36)?[111] Trudeau's satire attacked the televangelist playbook of putting money and religion in stark relationship.

While Garry Trudeau did not draw the Oral Roberts University campus in connection to the "Oral Roberts Death Watch," the architecture of the campus once again played host to the drama of Roberts's visions. This time, the Prayer Tower on the campus became the central focus. In a ten-day stretch in late March 1987 marking the end of his vigil over his life, Oral Roberts reportedly sequestered himself in his prayer room located on the observation level of the Prayer Tower, though the press was kept away from the tower.[112] That Roberts was secluded in vigil in the Prayer Tower, in communion with God praying fervently for donations at the threat of his own life, put the purpose of the Prayer Tower and the core beliefs of Oral Roberts on full display. While Roberts's faith seemed to be affirmed once again

**Figure 36.** *Doonesbury* cartoon by Garry Trudeau depicting the "Oral Roberts Death Watch," February 5, 1987. (DOONESBURY © 1987 G. B. Trudeau; Reprinted with permission of ANDREWS MCMEEL SYNDICATION; All rights reserved)

in this case—he raised a full $9 million for his medical ministries by late March 1987, and God did not call Roberts home until three decades later in 2009—the success was temporary. Oral Roberts closed the City of Faith buildings in 1989 due to massive debt, and the renamed and secularized CityPlex Towers are now used for commercial offices. We can understand the City of Faith and the Prayer Tower at Oral Roberts University as landscapes of sincere faith that also became landscapes of doubt questioning Pentecostal belief.

The iconic image of Jerry Falwell's slide down the Heritage USA waterslide, *The Simpsons'* Praiseland cartoon parody of Heritage USA, the altered photograph of Oral Roberts University's City of Faith buildings warning of a 900-foot Jesus crossing, and the "Oral Roberts Death Watch" connected to Roberts's prayer vigil in the Prayer Tower are powerful visual critiques of American televangelism and Pentecostalism. They were not the only satires at the time. Ted Koppel's "Billion Dollar Pie" televised report in 1987 made a biting critique of televangelists' enormous sums of money. Larry Flynt, publisher of the sexually explicit *Hustler* magazine, satirized Jerry Falwell in a crude 1983 faux advertisement undermining Falwell's moral beliefs, leading to the 1988 United States Supreme Court decision in *Hustler Magazine v. Jerry Falwell* that affirmed Flynt's ability to parody public figures. Several plays and musicals based on Tammy Faye Bakker's life have been both proposed and performed, with their advertisements often highlighting her iconic running mascara in another visual satire, this time of the female body.[113]

The satire of the evangelical theme park continues. In his 2008 mockumentary *Religulous,* comedian Bill Maher featured the Holy Land Experience park in Orlando, Florida, where he asks the man performing as Jesus in the Passion play why God would allow the Holocaust.[114] As the cameras film the play, they capture the moment when, just as Jesus is crucified on the cross, a plane passes overhead, underscoring the incongruous juxtaposition of a reenacted two-thousand-year-old event removed from its historic time and place and positioned in a land of amusement. In the same mockumentary, Maher also visited the Creation Museum in Petersburg, Kentucky, opened in 2007 by the Answers in Genesis organization. As chapter 4 explores, the Creation Museum and its sister park the Ark Encounter, opened in 2016 also in Kentucky, are fundamentalist theme parks also subjected to visual forms of satire and critique. Jim Bakker has made his Morningside Church in Blue Eye, Missouri (only thirty minutes from tourist mecca Branson, Missouri) a reincarnated Heritage USA, with a Grace Street mirroring Heritage USA's Main Street; a General Store; "The Tabernacle," a version of Heritage USA's Upper Room Chapel; "Lori's House," a home for pregnant women much like Heritage USA's Heritage House; an RV park; condos and other rental facilities; a School of Media; and studio space for the televised *The Jim Bakker Show.* Morningside Church, too, has drawn ridicule from outsiders, this time for Jim Bakker's claim of a coming apocalypse and his selling of overpriced water and food to doomsday preparers.[115]

The meaning of the evangelical theme park has been transformed by religious doubt and satire. While Heritage USA crafted a place of Christian community and recreation and while Oral Roberts University created a permanent religious world's fair, their connection to televangelists who were fallible humans, in the case of Jim Bakker, and made extraordinary claims, in the case of Oral Roberts, made them objects of religious satire. It is significant that the campuses and buildings of these two televangelical empires were embedded in these satires. The physical structures of Heritage USA and Oral Roberts University made visible the beliefs of these Pentecostal preachers—a life infused with Jesus at every point. Heritage USA and Oral Roberts University were and are evidence of the supernatural in the world to believers. The religious satires of them expressed doubt and discomfort at this idea that God and Jesus are present in the world at all times, engaged in human concerns such as money and entertainment.

# 4

## CHARLES DARWIN'S NIGHT AT THE CREATION MUSEUM

On its list of "The Dumbest People, Events and Things of 2007," the satirical publication *MAD* magazine included the Creation Museum in Petersburg, Kentucky, just twenty minutes outside of Cincinnati, Ohio (fig. 37).[1] The Creation Museum, and now the Ark Encounter theme park featuring a life-size Noah's Ark in nearby Williamstown, Kentucky, are the signature architectural projects of Answers in Genesis, a Christian fundamentalist group founded in 1994, with roots in 1980, headed by Ken Ham. Answers in Genesis advocates Young Earth creationism, a set of beliefs that the Bible is to be understood literally as the true, inerrant word of God; that the Earth is about 6,000 years old according to the timeline in the Book of Genesis in contrast to the 4.5 billion years old held by consensus science; that God created the Earth and all its inhabitants, including humans and dinosaurs contemporaneously, in 6 contiguous 24-hour days; that the great flood described in the Book of Genesis was a global event that wiped out everything except for the life preserved on the ark (8 humans and 1,400 kinds of animals) and that science, framed in terms of the historical versus the observational, can prove it; and that Charles Darwin's theory of evolution is very, very wrong.[2] Accompanying the satirical honor granted by *MAD* magazine was a parody cartoon titled "Charles Darwin's Night at the Creation Museum," a play on the movie poster for the 2006 film *Night at the Museum.* As we will see, the image caustically doubted the Creation Museum's belief in creationism and denial of consensus science.

Reactions to the Creation Museum and the Ark Encounter fall toward the extreme end of the spectrum of religious satire directed at religious buildings. "Touchdown Jesus" at the University of Notre Dame is received as endearing by both insiders and outsiders, and Jerry

**Figure 37.** Creation Museum in Petersburg, Kentucky, opened in 2007. (AP Photo/Ed Reinke)

Falwell himself recognized the satirical image of his fall down the waterslide. The satires aligning the Mormon Washington D.C. Temple to *The Wizard of Oz* and ridiculing Oral Roberts's 900-foot Jesus in the City of Faith more bitingly questioned religious belief. Yet each of these satires still possessed an air of levity in the exchange that offered an invitation to encounter the religious other. The satires of the Creation Museum and the Ark Encounter are sharper and darker with little room for negotiation. While Answers in Genesis sees the Creation Museum and the Ark Encounter as places for evangelical outreach (the Creation Museum's slogan is "Prepare to Believe," and Answers in Genesis "urge[s] atheists, even those who are the most hostile toward Christianity, and people of all other faiths, to visit our attractions, for our Ark Encounter and Creation Museum are all about proclaiming the vital message that the Bible is true from the very first verse"[3]), they are also strident warnings of what it means not to believe in God's literal word. Those who believe in other mechanisms for creation—for example, Old Earth creationism, theistic evolution, or atheistic Darwinism—that do not follow the narrative told in the Book of Genesis stand in opposition to the fundamentalist belief of Answers in Genesis. The 2014 National Study of Religion and Human Origins found that 37 percent of adult Americans consider themselves creationists in a broad sense— with only 8 percent upholding more restrictive beliefs about creationism like Answers in Genesis—and that 16 percent believe in theistic evolution and 9 percent in atheistic evolution.[4] The acceptance of Darwinian evolution and consensus science dominates American secular and popular culture, positioning the Creation Museum and the Ark Encounter as places for confrontation. Answers in Genesis expects hostile and satirical responses from skeptics. On the Creation Museum's entry door is a sign that warns, "Loud, disrespectful, disruptive, obscene or abusive behavior will not be tolerated, and any persons engaging in such conduct or wearing clothing or items that are offensive to other guests and to our staff will be subject to removal from the premises."

*MAD* magazine's caustic parody seems to easily dismiss the beliefs of Answers in Genesis, with its depiction of humans existing alongside dinosaurs framed not just as doubtful but absurd. Such responses aim to put the museum on the cultural fringe of America. The Creation Museum and the Ark Encounter proactively anticipate this doubting and make an unshakable assertion that it is those who do not believe in creationism and biblical inerrancy who are the foolish ones. As Susan and William Trollinger—scholars writing from the position of outsider and skeptic—argue in their analysis of the Creation Museum, we should not "dismiss the Creation Museum as a surreal oddity, an inexplicable and bizarre cultural site," or "a wacky but essential irrelevant outpost on the far outskirts of America life." The Trollingers see the museum as something to be taken seriously "because it presents and speaks to the religious and political commitments of a large swath of the American population" and "seeks to shape, prepare, and arm millions of American Christians as uncompromising and fearless warriors for what it understands to be the ongoing culture war in America."[5] The Creation Museum and the Ark Encounter frankly assert that it is the nonbelievers, not the believers in Young Earth creationism, who face the dire consequence of not being saved for all eternity. They offer not just one plausible structure of religious belief in a pluralistic nation—theirs is the one and only religious belief that leads to salvation. The Creation Museum and the Ark Encounter are judging you, and they do not particularly care if you are judging them.

### The Creation Museum

Opened in 2007, the Creation Museum is the explicit material realization—spatial, architectural, visual, and written—of the fundamentalist beliefs of Answers in

Genesis and its leader Ken Ham. Ham, born in Australia to parents who believed in creationism, was a science teacher who started a ministry advocating the truth of the creation of the world as presented in the Book of Genesis. He immigrated to the United States in 1987.[6] Ham and Answers in Genesis have stated publicly that they located their headquarters in northern Kentucky just outside Cincinnati for the reason that nearly two-thirds of the United States population, in their estimation, were within a 650-mile radius and therefore readily accessible to its evangelical message,[7] but implicit in their decision to locate their outreach in Kentucky is the state's strong conservative identity and large evangelical Christian population. By 2015, over 2.5 million people had visited the Creation Museum, though most of these were in the museum's early years.[8] As scholars have argued, the Creation Museum employs visual, written, and verbal techniques to undermine dominant scientific credibility and to craft the legitimacy of its own worldview. It also offers a dark assessment of contemporary culture and issues a warning for society to reform its ways or face the wrath of God, just like the flood in Noah's time. The message of the Creation Museum is twofold: that the Bible is the literal truth of the word of God, and that there is safety and security in obeying God and destruction and death for those who do not. More than a museum, I argue, the Creation Museum is perhaps best thought of as the megachurch of Answers in Genesis.

The Creation Museum is a physical manifestation of Christian fundamentalist beliefs that God and Jesus are the sole path of salvation for a world that cyclically shows corruption of sin and judgment for that sin. Christian fundamentalism arose out of Charles Darwin's 1859 *On the Origin of Species* and the movement of historicism, which challenged the truth of the Bible.[9] Within the Christian fundamentalist tradition, Ken Ham and Answers in Genesis have an organizing worldview that recalls, but does not exactly replicate, dispensational premillennialism, a belief developed in the 1830s and made widely known by the 1909 *Scofield Reference Bible* that the Bible tells not just the story of the past but also foretells humanity's future. Dispensational premillennialists emphasize the Book of Revelation and the Book of Daniel; the rapture, or the second coming of Jesus Christ on Earth; the realization of the City of God on Earth; the end of times; and the trials to be encountered with the devil before then in seven dispensations or eras of history. The Creation Museum presents its own organizing worldview in terms of the seven *c*'s—creation (at the Garden of Eden), corruption (the fall of Adam), catastrophe (the great flood), confusion (confusing human language and scattering humans across the globe at the Tower of Babel), Christ (the coming of God in human form), cross (Christ's death for our salvation), and consummation (the coming of God again on Earth to remake it in perfection, without sin)—that, as the Trollingers argue, has simplified a narrative of the world to one about God's command, man's disobedience to that command, and God's punishment ("command, disobedience, punishment"), a narrative that becomes the museum's organizational structure.[10] Ham and Answers in Genesis believe that the contemporary world, much like the world in the time of Noah, is going down the wrong path. Two much-studied exhibits of the museum, Graffiti Alley (which aligns urban architectural forms to societal sin) and Culture in Crisis, give grave warnings about abortion, gay marriage, euthanasia, teen pregnancy, violence, drug use, and pornography.[11] In contrast to secular natural history museums, the Creation Museum tells a story that is dark and repetitive, not one of progress.[12] At the end of the museum's exhibits, visitors enter a theater to view *The Last Adam* movie (notably filmed at the Holy Land Experience theme park in Orlando, Florida) interwoven with images of blood and fire that tells the story of Jesus's life, crucifixion, and resurrection to make the claim to museum visitors that belief in Jesus Christ—the last Adam—is the path to salvation.[13] The museum's focus on the flood and Noah's Ark is a way to tell visitors that just as God judged and punished the world in the time of Noah with the great flood, God will do so again in our time.[14] To be saved from death and destruction, the Creation Museum tells its visitors, we must be obedient to God's word as told in the Bible.[15]

The Creation Museum's exposition and defense of biblical inerrancy generates the museum's exhibits that those who do not believe in a literal reading of the Bible find fantastic and unbelievable. If the Bible is to be understood literally, then humans and dinosaurs would have coexisted in the same era, a belief that goes against claims of consensus science that dinosaurs lived some 66 million years before humans. A diorama near the Creation Museum's entrance shows young children playing peacefully alongside dinosaurs, and dinosaurs are present in the room-size diorama of the Garden of Eden (fig. 38). The museum's Dragon Hall Bookstore furthers the claims about the existence of dinosaurs in the era of humans, arguing that fire-breathing dragons depicted in medieval knight stories and other

**Figure 38.** A diorama exhibit in the Creation Museum that suggests dinosaurs and humans coexisted in the same time period. (Jim West/ Alamy Stock Photo)

stories from the eighth to nineteenth centuries were actually dinosaurs.[16] In keeping with the Bible's record of the first humans (Adam and Eve) and the story of Cain and Abel (the museum includes a diorama with a figure of Cain over Abel's dead body), the Creation Museum includes an explanatory plaque that answers its stated question, "Where did Cain get his wife?," frankly admitting and defending the necessity of the incestuous relationship between Cain and mostly likely his sister to propagate the human race said in the Bible to be descended solely from Adam and Eve. Another animatronic display of Noah's grandfather Methuselah, a bridge figure who, we are told in Genesis, knew Adam and witnessed God's command to Noah to build the ark, asserts that Methuselah lived to be 969 years old as told in the timeline in Genesis, defying what consensus science understands the possible lifespan of humans to be. The display of a portion of Noah's Ark in the Creation Museum (anticipating the later realization of the full-scale ark at the Ark Encounter) is the culmination of Answers in Genesis's core beliefs, asserting the great flood described in the Book Genesis was a real, global event occurring about 6,000 years ago, wiping out all life save for the eight humans and 1,400 "kinds" of animals (a category broader than species). This flood event, they claim, generated the world's fossils. Consensus science holds that there is no geological evidence of a global flood nearly 6,000 years ago, that the fossil record is much older than 6,000 years, and that Earth's biodiversity could not have derived from the animals (and humans) said to be saved on the ark. In its adherence to the events told in the Bible, the Creation Museum crafts a narrative of its view of how the world came to be and carefully constructs explanations for contrary arguments.

Rather than running away from science, the Creation Museum, Answers in Genesis, and Ken Ham run headlong toward it, recasting the very nature of "science" as a way to defend its belief in biblical inerrancy. Ken Ham argues that "science" exists in two senses: observational and historical. For Ham, observational science is conducted in the present according to the scientific method and is repeatable by other scientists. Historical science, on the other hand, is by its very nature based in history and therefore is not subject to firsthand experience or testing by the scientific method. Without the ability to observe it directly, historical science, like evolution, relies on a set of assumptions. For Ham, "whereas observational science is objective, historical science is not."[17] In framing science between observational (the objective) and historical (the subjective), Ham is able to cast doubt on the accuracy of evolution and cultivate creationism as a plausible alternative given that we cannot directly observe creation located in the past.[18] In their examination of the Creation Museum, again from the position of outsider and skeptic, Casey Ryan Kelly and Kristen E. Hoerl argue that the entire aim of the museum is "to delegitimize scientific authority."[19] They argue that the Creation Museum presents a "pseudoscientific alternative to natural history by staging a *disingenuous* or *manufactured* controversy between evolution and creationism" with a goal "to cultivate doubt in the public" about evolution.[20] To this point, the museum's opening exhibits in the "Bible Walkthrough Experience" pit a scientist who believes in evolution against a scientist who is open to the ideas of creationism, immediately situating the museum visitor within a narrative of doubt about one authoritative way to view natural history evidence.

Even as it seeks to undermine consensus science, the Creation Museum appropriates the architectural language, exhibit methods, and even naming of secular natural history museums to garner the trust and authority these institutions enjoy in American society. In calling itself a "museum," the Creation Museum aligns itself with other cultural institutions. The Creation Museum places itself specifically within the category of natural history museums such as the American Museum of Natural History in New York City, the Field Museum of Natural History in Chicago, and the Smithsonian National Museum of Natural History in Washington, D.C., as an authentic and authoritative collector, guardian, and interpreter of the Earth's natural history. The Creation Museum employs the interpretive techniques of the natural history museum, including display of objects under glass, dioramas with life-size human and animal figures, tags with scientific and common names of specimens, and explanatory plaques.[21] Answers in Genesis appropriates scientific authority in other ways. It publishes what it calls a scientific journal, *Answers Research Journal,* echoing peer-reviewed scientific journals, but as the Trollingers have pointed out, its articles are authored repeatedly by a small number of people and do not conform to typical standards of secular scientific journals.[22] In aligning itself with the techniques and structures of secular scientific institutions, the Creation Museum co-opts their credibility, respectability, and authority.

The Creation Museum's architecture also appropriates the language of modern museum and cultural institutions, but this architecture gives us clues for understanding the building not only as a museum but also as a megachurch. The museum's design, led by architect George Nielsen of A. M. Kinney Associates based in Cincinnati, has a rather anonymous exterior.[23] A concave colonnade encased in dark glass and topped by a visually heavy, unornamented cornice dominates the museum's entrance as battered stone sidewalls and landscaping mask the museum's massive 75,000-square-foot volume (see fig. 37). The clues to the building's identity are not given by the architecture itself but rather added symbols, including the dinosaur statues on the entrance plaza and the metal *Stegosaurus* on the entrance sign visible from the main road. But if we put aside the dinosaur forms and ignore the building's name for a moment, the building comes into view as something else. A. A. Gill, a British writer, described the museum's architecture in an overtly satirical *Vanity Fair* article entitled "Roll Over, Charles Darwin!" this way: "Oddly, it is a conspicuously and emphatically secular construction. There is no religious symbolism. No crosses. No stained glass. No spiral campanile. It has borrowed the empirical vernacular of the enemy to wrap the literal interpretation of Genesis in the façade of a liberal art gallery or library. It is the Lamb dressed in wolf's clothing."[24] Gill's impulse to want to see the building in the form of a church is telling. For him, because the Creation Museum is a testament of faith rather than secular, scientific consensus, it should take the form of a church with hallmark crosses, stained glass, and campanile. What

Gill got right is that we can indeed view the Creation Museum as a church, but what he got wrong was what the architecture of the contemporary American fundamentalist and evangelical church looks like. We can read the Creation Museum as the form of the Protestant megachurch in addition to its identity as a museum. The very use of anonymous or secular architecture devoid of overt religious symbolism is a hallmark of the American megachurch, which appeals to forms of the shopping mall and vernacular commercial spaces as a way to make people feel invited and not threatened.[25] While the Creation Museum does not have regular religious services in the way a megachurch would, it does attract large numbers of people, and it is a place for religious instruction. For Gill, the building's architectural appearance as a "façade of a liberal art gallery or library"—by which he means an architecture of secular cultural institutions—means it is "the Lamb dressed in wolf's clothing" (and note here Gill's witty play on the familiar idiom with "Lamb" capitalized to be understood as Jesus) in the sense of tricking people into believing the building is a secular museum when in fact it is a place of religious faith. While Answers in Genesis operates as a parachurch ministry, the Creation Museum, and now also the Ark Encounter, are its architectural statements of faith in the same way as a Protestant megachurch. In this understanding, the Creation Museum is more than our traditional conception of a museum.

In his satirical account, A. A. Gill used a critique of architecture to cultivate doubt about the Creation Museum and the believability of the faith it asserted. Calling the Creation Museum a "tacky, risible, and rational tableau," Gill dismissed it as "irredeemably kitsch" and guessed that "it may be the biggest collection of kitsch in God's entire world." Gill made an aesthetic judgment of the museum's material and visual expressions of faith: the Creation Museum was a "cheap county-fair sideshow" that could not compete with "the creation story in Michelangelo's Sistine Chapel, Masaccio's expulsion from Eden, or any of the thousands of flickering images, icons, and installations based on faith rather than literalist realism." For Gill, the museum's literalism—which is the entire foundation of creationist belief—found in its corporate-feeling architecture, in its displays of Adam and Eve alongside dinosaurs, and in its interpretative signs that carefully counter alternative ways to see the world removes any sense of the religious imagination and any feeling of the transcendental. The museum, Gill wrote, "is the profound represented by the banal" that actually "defies belief, beggars faith."[26] Gill fails to see the ways that religious kitsch—whether we use that term in a neutral sense, as Frank Burch Brown does in his book *Good Taste, Bad Taste, and Christian Taste,* or in a derisive sense, as Gill does—can be appealing to people's religious and spiritual sensibilities.[27] Clearly, the Creation Museum fails to speak to Gill and others who see it as too literal to be transcendental, but it does speak to some people for whom the divine can be found in the literal and even in the banal.

The Creation Museum turns the tables on religious doubt we have seen throughout this book. Rather than passive acceptors of a dominant culture's skepticism, the Creation Museum and now the Ark Encounter willingly engage in the debate between creationism and evolution, cultivating doubt about consensus science. As James Bielo argues, in the Creation Museum and the Ark Encounter "creationists work to sow suspicion about the cultural legitimacy of evolutionary science and bolster the status of fundamentalist Christianity."[28] While some see the Creation Museum as foolish, the Creation Museum and Answers in Genesis are openly willing to call those who do not believe in biblical inerrancy the foolish ones.

## Charles Darwin at the Creation Museum

On February 4, 2014, in the Creation Museum's 1,500-seat Legacy Hall, Ken Ham of Answers in Genesis and Bill Nye, best known for his 1990s television show *Bill Nye the Science Guy,* debated the question "Is creation a viable model of origins in today's modern scientific era?" The two-and-a-half hour debate that pitted evolution against creationism attracted wide attention. It was broadcast live on the internet with audience figures estimated between 500,000 and 5 million, and the YouTube video of the debate has gathered more than 7 million views as of 2019.[29] Later in 2014, Bill Nye published the book *Undeniable: Evolution and the Science of Creation* spurred by his experience at the debate, which he recounted in an early chapter titled "The Great Creationism Debate."[30] Ken Ham framed the debate as "Scopes II," in his view a vindication for the outcome of the 1925 Scopes Trial where science teacher John Scopes was put on trial for violating Tennessee's law prohibiting the teaching of evolution in public schools, a trial made famous in the 1955 play and 1960 movie *Inherit the Wind.* At the 1925 trial, William Jennings Bryan took the stand in defense of creationism, but under questioning he did not fully support a literal reading of Genesis.[31] At the 2014 debate, Ken Ham vigorously defended creationism against Nye's stance on evolution, putting to rest concerns from some creationist Christians that they "would look like backwaters fools who knew nothing of science, who equivocated on the age of the Earth, and, even worse, wavered on the literal meaning of Genesis."[32] As the *Daily Beast's* Michael Schulson wrote, "if you listened closely, what Ham was saying made absolutely no scientific sense. But debate is a format of impressions, not facts. Ham *sounded* like a reasonable human being, loosely speaking, and that's what mattered."[33] Ham's performance at the debate was just part of the Creation Museum's larger mission to reverse how creationism has been portrayed in broader American culture.[34] As Ham said, the Scopes Trial "was the first time the Bible was ridiculed by the media in America, and that was a downward turning point for Christendom. We are going to undo all of that here at the Creation Museum. We are going to answer the questions Bryan wasn't prepared to, and show that belief in every word of the Bible can be defended by modern science."[35]

Ken Ham and Bill Nye's 2014 debate at the Creation Museum recalled the original evolution-creationism debate ("debate" as commonly described, but "exchange" as corrected by scholars) at another museum of natural history: the Bishop Samuel Wilberforce and Thomas Huxley exchange in 1860 at the Oxford University Museum of Natural History in England. There, in the museum's west room during the meeting of the British Association for the Advancement of Science, an American scientist named John William Draper gave a paper on Charles Darwin's *On the Origin of Species,* published in 1859 (Darwin himself was absent from the meeting due to illness). In the discussion following Draper's remarks, the sharp exchange remembered in history between Wilberforce, a bishop in the Church of England, and Huxley, a scientist who came to be known as "Darwin's bulldog," centered on the idea that if Darwin's theory of natural selection were correct, that would mean that humans were not put on Earth as described in the Book of Genesis but rather descended from apes—an idea that Darwin had not actually emphasized in *On the Origin of Species* (though he would in his 1872 *Descent of Man*), but one that had captured the public's imagination and become a talking point in the press.[36] Wilberforce vehemently did not believe in this lineage. He asserted to the gathered scientists, "The line between man and the lower animals was distinct; there was no tendency on the part of lower animals to become the self-conscious intelligent being, man; or in man to degenerate and lose the high characteristics of his mind and intelligence . . . Mr. Darwin's conclusions were an hypothesis, raised most unphilosophically to the dignity of a casual theory."[37] Some accounts record a more biting, satirical exchange between Wilberforce and Huxley that made this idea of the descent from apes highly personal and therefore memorable. As Carla Yanni recounts in her history of natural history museums, "One account has it that Wilberforce asked Huxley if he descended from apes on his grandfather's or grandmother's side, and Huxley responded that he would sooner be descended from an ape than from a 'divine who employ[ed] authority to stifle the truth.'"[38] Huxley's own version was that if the question were put to him "would I rather have a miserable ape for a grandfather or a man highly endowed by nature and possessed of great means and influence and yet who employs those faculties for the mere purpose of introducing ridicule into a grave scientific discussion, I unhesitatingly affirm my preference for the ape."[39] Wilberforce's clear religious affiliation and Huxley's publicly avowed agnosticism and opposition to organized religion overlaid questions about religious belief onto this question about the origin of humans.

Just as the Creation Museum figured prominently as the setting for the Ken Ham and Bill Nye debate, so too did the Oxford University Museum of Natural History figure prominently as the backdrop between Wilberforce and Huxley's exchange on the origin of humans. In both cases, the setting was far from neutral. The Oxford University Museum of Natural History—a Venetian Gothic revival structure designed by the Irish architects Deane and Woodward, influenced directly by John Ruskin, and completed in 1860—joined science and religion visually, materially, and architecturally.[40] As Carla Yanni argues, the Oxford museum "was meant to be a place where students could contemplate authentic physical wonders of Nature and the greatness of godly design."[41] As such, the building itself became a record of the natural world, an architectural revelation of nature's—and God's—design. Carved in the building itself, both in stone and in the remarkable cast iron columns, were flora from various epochs and geographies as its halls and rooms displayed dinosaur skeletons and other natural specimens. The museum's iconic and innovative glass atrium—modeled after Joseph Paxton's glass pavilion for the 1851 Great Exhibition in London and believed to be the first use of extensive glass and steel for a cultural institution—was shaped by pointed arches recalling a Gothic church nave (fig. 39). Carved within the museum's entrance arch are the figures of Adam and Eve, fruit and thorns, and an angel at the arch's apex. The angel holds a book representing the intellectual and spiritual life in one hand and a dividing nucleated cell representing the material life in the other, imagery that, as Yanni interprets, "combines, rather than distinguishes, spirituality and materiality."[42] This image of a natural science museum housed within a building with ecclesiastical references was far from jarring for a Victorian culture that put science and religion not in opposition but rather in harmony embedded in the idea of natural theology—the idea that if the Bible was God's first book, nature was his second.[43] Darwin's ideas and writings accelerated the cleaving of science from religion, making him an icon of secular science, and yet Darwin is materially present in the Oxford museum where religion and science remain fused. His crustacean specimens gathered during his famed 1830s voyage on *The Beagle* are included in the museum's collection, and an 1899 statue of Charles Darwin by sculptor Henry Hope Pinker is on display in the glass and iron courtyard alongside statues of Aristotle, Galileo, Isaac Newton, and Carl Linnaeus (fig. 40).

**Figure 39.** Interior of the Oxford University Museum of Natural History, architects Deane and Woodward, Oxford, England, 1855–60. (David Jones/Alamy Stock Photo)

Charles Darwin has a place in the Oxford University Museum of Natural History, which positions him within a longer history of using science to understand God's design, but in its literal understanding of Genesis, the Creation Museum has no place for Charles Darwin.

This understanding of Charles Darwin—his origin with a Victorian culture sympathetic to natural theology, his connection to the Oxford University Museum of Natural History and the famous discussion of his ideas there, and his later transformation into an icon of secular science—is central to understanding the satire of the Creation Museum inherent in the 2008 image "Charles Darwin's Night at the Creation Museum" in *MAD* magazine.[44] Importantly, DC Entertainment, which controls the copyright of *MAD* magazine, declined permission for the image "Charles Darwin's Night at the Creation Museum" to be reproduced in this book, but readers can readily find the image on the internet to follow along in this analysis. The cartoon features a terrified Charles Darwin, dressed in a suit with waistcoat clutching his white hair with both hands, his mouth

**Figure 40.** Statue of Charles Darwin (1899) by sculptor Henry Hope Pinker in the Oxford University Museum of Natural History. (Bigred/ Alamy Stock Photo)

open in the gesture of a yell, his legs and body in the posture of running out of the museum, which we are to understand as the architecture of the Creation Museum (though in reality it is not). The Charles Darwin of the mid-nineteenth-century Victorian culture would not have been terrified by the Creation Museum's focus on the creation story told in the Bible, but the Charles Darwin made into a symbol for our contemporary culture in which science and religion have been cast as binaries is clearly terrified. This caricature of Charles Darwin serves the satire's purpose well. Charles Darwin becomes the proxy for the viewer without the viewer's choice. Like Darwin, we too are running away from creationism, whose beliefs are caricatured in the image to seem maximally preposterous.

The "Charles Darwin's Night at the Creation Museum" parody makes a series of humorous and caustic visual substitutions within the frame of the promotional poster for the 2006 movie *Night at the Museum*. The parody image assumes the setting from the movie poster, a hallway lined with classical pilasters in alternating colored stone. (The *Night at the Museum* sets were patterned after the American Museum of Natural History in New York City, whose architecture evolved with a series of additions from Victorian Gothic to neo-Romanesque to Beaux-Arts styles.) The terrified Charles Darwin takes the place of actor Ben Stiller, who plays a museum night watchman in the movie, as the image's dominant figure, backlit by a strong, golden glow. By purposeful contrast to the terrified Darwin, the other figures in the parody image, composed in vignettes that substitute the characters depicted in the movie poster, are relaxed and comfortable within the Creation Museum since they support creationist belief. In the image's left foreground and at miniature (recalling the miniature warring armies in the movie poster), pairs of giraffes, penguins, elephants, cows, kangaroos, and even unicorns arrive on Noah's Ark as a figure of Noah, alongside his wife, raises his arms in an appeal to listen to the Lord and the coming flood. Just behind the ark, a miniature pair of dragons, one with smoke coming out of its mouth, attests to the creationist belief that dragons were dinosaurs alive at the time of humans. The coexistence of dinosaurs and humans is a belief made at a larger scale in the image, as a giant but rather domesticated *Tyrannosaurus rex* in the flesh (a nod to the skeleton of the *Tyrannosaurus rex* fondly nicknamed Rexy from the movie poster) gives a ride to a bearded and robed Moses, recognizable with the two tablets of the Ten Commandments from God and his staff in hand. Other dinosaurs populate the image on the right side: a *Pterodactyl* flies above a *Triceratops,* led on a leash by a monkey (recalling the monkey Dexter in the movie), a primate in the same taxonomic order as humans satirically implying human's evolution even within this creationist scene. Within this exposition of dinosaurs, we see a smiling Adam, presumably naive and clothed only with a leaf, reaching his hand out to happily accept the apple from a similarly nude Eve at the very moment before the fall, the original sin. In this one image, the *MAD* magazine caricature visually summarizes key components of Young Earth creationism's literal reading of the Book of Genesis and, in Darwin's reaction to these beliefs, asserts their absurdity.

One final component of the *MAD* magazine satirical cartoon—a sign of "TRUTH" overcoming "DARWIN"—encapsulates the creationism and evolution debate in a familiar image from American material religion and popular culture. Hanging from the museum's

ceiling in the image is a decal, typically seen affixed to the back of a car, of the word "TRUTH" inscribed within the shape of an ichthys, the Greek word for fish, that early Christians used as a secret symbol for Jesus (fig. 41). This larger "TRUTH" fish devours a smaller fish shape (notably with feet) inscribed with the word "DARWIN," a symbol of evolution. "TRUTH" eating "DARWIN" was a creationist rebuke of evolution—here "TRUTH" in the sense of revealed knowledge overcomes secular knowledge. This vignette is only one part of a visual war among these symbols. In American car culture, we see also decals of only the ichthys representing the belief in Christ, decals of only the fish with "DARWIN" and feet representing evolution, and paired decals where the "DARWIN" fish eats the fish representing Christ. In these various permutations on the back of cars, on American highways and roads, a visual war of belief plays out in full public view. *MAD* magazine's inclusion of these signs acknowledges their widespread use in American culture and is a witty way to convey the back-and-forth public debate where one side claims victory over the other in a zero-sum game.

While the visual image of the *MAD* magazine parody of the Creation Museum clearly satirizes creationist belief in a humorous way, the text accompanying the image takes the satire to an extreme. Under the headline "You Can't Darwin 'Em All," the magazine states this rationale for choosing the Creation Museum as number 14 of 20 on its list of "The Dumbest People, Events and Things of 2007":

> Finally there is compelling evidence that the theory of Evolution is wrong! For proof positive that man's intelligence has not evolved in eons, consider the Cro-Magnon brained imbeciles behind the recently opened Creation Museum in Petersburg, Kentucky. The museum's exhibits don't merely chal-

**Figure 41.** Graphic representation of the evolution debate playing on the Christian ichthys fish symbol, where Christian "truth" overcomes Charles Darwin's evolved footed fish, sometimes seen as a car decal. (Illustration Collection/Alamy Stock Photo)

lenge science, they ignore it completely! It's the only place in the world you can see man riding bareback on a dinosaur—except, of course, in an old episode of *The Flintstones.*

Dripping with sarcasm and outright ridicule, the magazine undercuts any claims the museum makes about science; aligns the museum with a children's cartoon about a fictitious prehistoric family and invokes the idea of humans domesticating dinosaurs; and insults the intelligence level of creationists. It is an extreme satire directed at the Creation Museum and Answers in Genesis.

Just how public we can consider this parody of the Creation Museum is challenged by the limited circulation of *MAD* magazine, which in 2007 and 2008 numbered between 175,000 and 200,000 subscribers and newsstand sales, far from its circulation peak of 2 million in the 1970s.[45] But *MAD* magazine, founded in 1952 and known for its humor by Jewish intellectuals, has a long history of parody in American culture whose influence extends beyond these subscription numbers.[46] This particular image castigating the Creation Museum is present on the internet, posted on sharable image websites such as Pinterest, and cited by scholars.[47] "Charles Darwin's Night at the Creation Museum," in both title and image, invokes American popular culture to create a biting account of the beliefs of Young Earth creationism embodied in the Creation Museum. This image represents a set of responses to the Creation Museum—satirical, humorous, and of simple disbelief— found in American culture.[48]

## The Fundamentalist Theme Park

The Creation Museum was only Answers in Genesis's first construction project (realized at $27 million in 2007), whose partial exhibit on Noah's Ark foreshadowed what was to come. In 2016, the organization completed the Ark Encounter in Williamstown, Kentucky, about a forty-five-minute drive from the Creation Museum, at a cost of $102 million and featuring a life-size re-creation of Noah's Ark amid a larger plan for other attractions on the site (fig. 42). If we can understand the Creation Museum as Answers in Genesis's megachurch, we can read the Ark Encounter as its fundamentalist theme park, a continuation of the evangelical theme park genre of

Heritage USA and Oral Roberts University we explored in chapter 3. James Bielo's detailed study of the making of the Ark Encounter reveals the ways that Answers in Genesis traffics in modern theme park strategies such as immersive play and a family-friendly approach but differs from the modern theme park's "capitalist consumption" purpose. Rather, Bielo argues, the Ark Encounter's aim is "devotional consumption" in service of its particular "religious pedagogy."[49] Together, the Creation Museum and the Ark Encounter locate Christian fundamentalist belief in the

**Figure 42.**
Re-creation of Noah's Ark at the Ark Encounter, Williamstown, Kentucky, opened 2016. (AP Photo/John Minchillo)

American landscape, realize these beliefs in visual and material ways, and attract visitors in fulfillment of its evangelical outreach mission. These physical places of belief make real the claims of the Bible and the literal authority of God's word through material religion, and they do so in ways that appeal to people's interest in popular culture and entertainment.

The Creation Museum and the Ark Encounter are biblical tourism and entertainment at its best. As James Bielo argues, "Entertainment, conceived as immersive play, is the engine that fuels the fun of Ark Encounter's fundamentalism."[50] In addition to multimedia exhibits, animatronic figures, and dioramas that animate Answers in Genesis's educational and religious message, the Creation Museum and the Ark Encounter also include landscapes of entertainment that appeal directly to children and to tourism in a broader sense. The entertainment landscape begun in the Creation Museum is magnified in the full theme park of the Ark Encounter. Outside the Creation Museum, crisscrossing the pond that separates the museum from its gardens, are the Screaming Raptor zip lines, but these are surpassed by the expanded Screaming Eagle zip line course at the Ark Encounter. The Creation Museum's Christmas Town, which features Garden of Lights and a live nativity, is again surpassed by the Ark Encounter's ChristmasTime exhibit with its "Encounter the Wonder" laser light show projected on the ark that tells the salvation story of Christ. The Creation Museum's small petting zoo is just a microcosm of the Ark Encounter's full Ararat Ridge Zoo, named for Mount Ararat in modern-day Turkey where the remains of Noah's Ark are said to be located. Both the Creation Museum and the Ark Encounter offer gift shops, a number of dining options, recreational vehicle parking, add-on packages for photography and events such as donkey rides, and multiday passes to both parks that identify them as places of entertainment and tourism. The state of Kentucky controversially granted tax incentives to the Ark Encounter for the tourism dollars and new jobs it brought to the state.

Answers in Genesis's future plans for the Ark Encounter confirm its ambition to be a religious Disneyland or Disney World in the way Jim Bakker planned for Heritage USA but was stopped short by scandal. Ham has planned a Tower of Babel to signify the hubris of humans; a Walled City; a First-Century Village; a "Journey Thru Biblical History" exhibit; a reported ten-plagues-of-Egypt thrill ride and

3,200-seat amphitheater; an unspecified "children's area"; and an aviary in addition to the zoo. Answers in Genesis frankly admits using the secular theme park as a model. As Ken Ham said, "How do you reach the general public in a bigger way? Why not attractions that people will come to the way they go to Disney or Universal or the Smithsonian?"[51] (However, Ham carefully emphasized the "religious purpose" of such an appeal in an interview with the *New York Times* a year earlier, saying, "The reason we are building the ark is not as an entertainment center. I mean it's not like a Disney or Universal, just for anyone to go and have fun. It's a religious purpose. It's because we're Christians and we want to get the Christian message out."[52]) In a description of the Ark Encounter, Mike Zovath, one of Ken Ham's partners, said, "Picture Disney Main Street with lots of shops, food and fun things to see," and Patrick Marsh, vice president of attractions design, confirmed this use of entertainment as a method of attraction: "if you want to attract people here, you need to do it at a Disney level. Kids are so used to high-quality things."[53]

The creators of the ark themselves saw it as a roadside attraction that could pay divine dividends. Ken Ham positioned the building of a gigantic ark as an act of faith: "You've got to be risk-takers to do something like this. But I see it as stepping out in faith. There are people you couldn't blow into church with a stick of dynamite that will come and visit an ark."[54] The novelty of a building one-and-a-half football fields in length and four stories high in the shape of an ark—a true architectural folly—was purposeful. Mike Zovath said their goal was for the ark to become "something on people's checklist when they're traveling, like seeing the biggest ball of twine. That gives us an opportunity for people who might never go to church to see something that is mind-blowing and get some information that could change their lives for the better and point them in the direction for a secure eternity."[55] Much like Heritage USA, the logic of the Ark Encounter and the Creation Museum is to meet people where they are and where they have an interest, which may well be outside a traditional church setting.

More than a merely curious roadside attraction, the ark is loaded with a religious worldview and political and social polemics. In his visit to the Ark Encounter in 2016, filmed as part of his 2017 documentary *Bill Nye: The Science Guy,* Bill Nye captured the ways that the ark is both an architectural folly and something more:

This could be just a charming piece of Americana, just something—I recently used an app called Roadtrippers that takes you to odd or unusual places . . . but this is much more serious than that. This guy [Ken Ham] promotes so very strongly that climate change is not a serious problem, that humans are not causing it, that some deity will see to it that everything is ok.[56]

The Ark Encounter, like the Creation Museum, is a public testament of religious belief, even in the form of a religious theme park, that is the architectural and material fulcrum around which debates about belief—in this case, about the truth of the Bible, about what we can know about the world through scientific methods, and about the concepts of creationism and evolution—are carried out.

### The Ark's Built Theology

The Ark Encounter's full-scale re-creation of Noah's Ark is the constructed theology of Answers in Genesis in the most vivid sense of material religion (see fig. 42). At 510 feet long and 51 feet high, the ark is a startling moment in the landscape, and purposefully so. Built entirely of wood, with the skill of Amish carpenters, and according to the dimensions in the Book of Genesis, the ark is a Christian fundamentalist warning of the judgment to come—a warning that is visible in the ark's very structure.

The ark re-creation is an architectural paradox of sculpture and building, boat and nonboat, form and function. The ark echoes the Big Duck on Long Island, New York, famously referenced in architects Robert Venturi, Denise Scott Brown, and Steven Izenour's *Learning from Las Vegas* (1972),[57] and it recalls the literalism of other buildings as advertisement, such as the Longaberger Company's former 1997 headquarters in Newark, Ohio, in the shape of a seven-story woven Longaberger basket. The re-created ark conveys an image of something it is really not. From the front, the building's carefully constructed primary view, the ark appears as a ship, a true ark. As visitors are told, the ark was constructed faithfully according to the description in Genesis, with exhibits explaining the translation of the cubit dimension found in the Bible to inches. The ark's dimensions are meant to be impressive, its very scale intended to convince visitors that this structure could hold two of every animal—and accommodate their practical needs—that would repopulate the Earth after the floodwaters receded. The pond placed between the ark and a viewing area allows the entire object to be taken in, to be seen as if it were floating on water, and, importantly, to be photographed in a manner designed to be impressive and to be shared with others (see fig. 42). But this view of the ark is a manufactured and manipulated image. The fiction of the ark's sculptural purity viewed from the front is betrayed by the rectangular structures on clear foundations on the backside of the ark that house mechanical systems, elevators, stairs, and bathrooms—the quotidian structures that signal that the ark is a building that must conform to modern codes and conveniences and very much is not floating anywhere.

Yet the very nonfloating nature of this re-created ark is an intentional, visible construction of fundamentalist Christian theology. Ark architect LeRoy Troyer, whose Indiana-based firm also planned the open-air museum Nazareth Village in Israel depicting a first-century Galilee village, said, "we built [the ark] specifically *not* to float." Troyer continued, "According to the Bible account, God said he'd never do a worldwide flood [again]."[58] The ark is a witness to a past event in support of the truth of the Bible, but it also has a pressing message for the present and the future. The massive expanse of the ark's port side is unrelentingly blank save for a singular feature: the door into the belly of the ship toward the bow. As journalist Amanda Petruish described it after viewing a scale model of the ark in 2012 (one wonders what her thought would be seeing the ark at full scale), the ark is terrifying in its blankness: "it is a terrifying-looking thing: it has no portholes or open decks, and except for a single door that God is supposed to have slammed behind Noah ('And Jehovah shut him in') and some very narrow openings for light and ventilation, the vessel is sealed off in a way that suggests a giant floating coffin."[59] In her reaction to the form of the ark, Petruish got at the purpose of the structure. The prominent, singular door is the culmination of the Answers in Genesis's theology about God's forthcoming judgment. Just as the people in Noah's time had a choice to turn toward God's word or dwell in sin, so too does our contemporary society have a choice to reject sin and turn toward God's will. In its Graffiti Alley exhibit at the Creation Museum, Answers in Genesis clearly outlines the vices of contemporary society it believes go against God's will: pornography, drug abuse, homosexuality, adultery, and removal of prayer from public school. At the Ark Encounter, the ark conveys the consequence of the choice to turn away from God's will: those who enter and accept God's word and are obedient to it will be saved; those who do not, who remain outside of the door and do not accept God's word, are subject to damnation. As a sign at the Ark Encounter titled "The Door" plainly states, "The Ark's door reminds us that we need to go through a door to be saved. Jesus Christ is our one door to salvation, the 'Ark' that saves us from God's judgment for eternity."[60] The door, the liminal space, is the moment of judgment. It represents a person's highly consequential and stark choice: inside or outside, inside God's graces or outside of them. The ark is a testament of faith in God, obedience to His word, and an expectation of judgment.[61]

This coming of moral judgment, recalled from the Book of Genesis and made present and pressing for modern times, is the message Answers in Genesis inscribes within the materiality of the ark re-creation. In appealing to notions of science as a way to prove that the biblical stories are real and that God indeed created the world as described in the Book of Genesis, Answers in Genesis seeks to confront a secular scientific world directly while transforming our understanding of what "science" means. But the irony, and humor, of Answers in Genesis eschewing the fruits of modern science in service of its theology was captured in a photograph at the time of the ark's construction (fig. 43). As the *New York Times* noted in 2016, when the shape of the ark was fully realized but before its exterior was sheathed in wood, the ark was wrapped with a common construction material called Tyvek, an envelope that protects buildings from the elements and boots energy efficiency, manufactured by the DuPont Company. The Tyvek wrap was emblazoned with DuPont's logo and its slogan, "The miracles of science," which was repeated not once but hundreds of times across the expanse of the ark's hull (fig. 44).[62] While the DuPont tagline does not foreclose entirely that God could be behind "The miracles of science," the slogan suggests that we are able to manufacture our own miracles based on an understanding of the natural world through human reason. "The miracles of science" tagline on the ark is humorous precisely for the incongruity of praising science within a creationist theme park that challenges consensus science. "The miracles of science" contradicted the miracles of God at root in Answers in Genesis theology and fundamentalist Christianity. Keeping with his rhetorical strategy of

**Figure 43.** Noah's Ark under construction, showing the Tyvek wrap printed with manufacturer DuPont's trademark, "The miracles of science." (KYLE GRILLOT/The New York Times/Redux)

meeting science on its own terms, in what the Trollingers call the "not-afraid-of-science Christian apologist," Ken Ham dismissed the incongruity of the slogan on the ark, writing on Twitter, "Some people scoff as we used Tyvek on Ark—of course we did! It's a wooden ship designed as a building for tourists," alongside his own photograph of the Tyvek-wrapped ark.[63] Yet the inclusion of "The miracles of science" slogan on the ark, though now hidden under the ark's wood sheathing, undercuts the ark's built theology as a challenge to the claims of modern science.

The Creation Museum and the Ark Encounter, which number among some thirty creationism-focused sites in the United States,[64] have visibility within American popular culture, appearing in a number of television shows from both supportive and satirical perspectives. The Duggar family from Arkansas, whose reality show focused on the supersized nature of their Christian fundamentalist family of nine-

teen children, visited the Creation Museum and met with Ken Ham on a 2008 episode of their program. The Duggars believe in creationism, and their encounter with Ken Ham at the Creation Museum was cast in a positive light (though how the viewers of this show perceived the Creation Museum is open to debate). Other television and film projects more frankly satirize Answers in Genesis and their parks. In 2017, Ozzy Osbourne and his son Jack visited the Ark Encounter as an American oddity as part of their *Ozzy and Jack's World Detour* program. Ozzy Osbourne, the former lead singer of the rock band Black Sabbath, has been aligned in popular culture as a Satanist (though Osbourne has denied this) who in his career famously bit the head off a dove and a bat. One headline about his visit to the Ark Encounter read, "Ozzy Visits the Ark Encounter and Doesn't Suffer the Wrath of God."[65] And as already mentioned, the Creation Museum and the Ark Encounter also appeared in the 2017 documentary *Bill Nye: The Science Guy,* where Bill Nye casts Answers in Genesis as "anti-science."[66]

**Figure 44.** Detail of the printing on Tyvek wrap on a residential home with DuPont's trademark "The miracles of science," which was also repeated hundreds of times on the Noah's Ark re-creation at the Ark Encounter. (Photograph by Margaret M. Grubiak)

The Creation Museum and the Ark Encounter are the megachurch and theme park of Answers in Genesis, the architectural and material realization of its belief in the fundamentalist view of Christianity. Because the Creation Museum and the Ark Encounter directly challenge evolution and consensus science, they are the locus for public debate and satire—ranging from humorous to hostile—in a culture where belief in consensus science seems to dominate. *MAD* magazine's caricature of "Charles Darwin's Night at the Creation Museum" co-opts American popular culture and a cultural construction of Charles Darwin to craft doubt about the beliefs that the Creation Museum and the Ark Encounter espouse. Yet Answers in

Genesis very much welcomes this debate, this satire, and even this hostility. Rather than a passive acceptor of satire directed at them, the Creation Museum and the Ark Encounter, in their very materiality, assert that those who do not believe are the foolish ones. Here the give-and-take of public debate over religious belief, and doubt, is on full display.

# 5

# GUMBY JESUS

A ubiquitous fixture of the American landscape, the giant Jesus image is a symbolic measure of faith: the 62-foot *King of Kings* statue off Interstate 75 in Ohio (fig. 45), whose upraised arms earned the nickname "Touchdown Jesus" much like the 134-foot *Word of Life* mural at the University of Notre Dame (see chapter 1); the 11-foot *Christus* statue in Mormon temple visitors' centers, including the one at the Washington D.C. Temple (see chapter 2); the 15-foot *Resurrected Christ* replica statue in Jim Bakker's Morningside Church in Missouri, the successor to his Heritage USA theme park (see chapter 3); the 900-foot Jesus preserved in the image of Oral Roberts's vision and the 900-foot Jesus crossing sign that began this book (see introduction and chapter 3); even the actor portrayal of Jesus as the "Last Adam" projected in superhuman size on the theater screen at the Creation Museum (see chapter 4).[1] The giant Jesus is a testament to his human and divine natures and an assertion of Jesus's continued presence in the world; it is an explicit expression of Christian theology. Yet as we have seen throughout this book, such assertions of faith are rarely received as intended or so simply construed. One more giant Jesus image — the 65.5-foot *Christ of the Ozarks* statue on Magnetic Mountain in Arkansas — crystalizes for us the complexity of landscapes of faith and doubt, where the drama

**Figure 45.** *King of Kings* statue (2004), also nicknamed "Touchdown Jesus," outside the Solid Rock Church, a Christian megachurch along Interstate 75 near Monroe, Ohio. The statue was destroyed by lightning in 2010 and replaced by another statue of Jesus, *Lux Mundi*, in 2012. (AP Photo/The Journal, Nick Graham)

over right and wrong belief plays out (fig. 46). While ostensibly a landscape of faith, the *Christ of the Ozarks* statue and its accompanying evangelical theme park were of a piece with its creator's anti-Semitic and racist beliefs, calling into question what it means when hate masquerades as religion. In this sense, the *Christ of the Ozarks* statue and its theme park are simultaneously landscapes of faith and doubt.

The *Christ of the Ozarks* statue that dominates the hilly terrain of Eureka Springs, Arkansas, is integral to the religious tourism landscape of the Ozarks, a common stop for those also on their way to see architect E. Fay Jones's nearby Thorncrown Chapel (1980).[2] At seven stories tall and visible up to twenty miles away, the white, boxy statue of Jesus with his arms outstretched in the shape of a cross, erected in 1966, recalls in general shape and color the 98-foot tall *Christ the Redeemer* statue (1922–31) in Rio de Janeiro, Brazil, another mountaintop statue famous as a symbol of its city, country, and Christianity writ large (fig. 47). The *Christ of the Ozarks* statue had similar ambitions as the first large-scale statue of Jesus in the United States. The man responsible for the statue, Gerald L. K. Smith, said, "my wife and I had been shocked down through the years that no one had ever lifted up a giant

**Figure 46.** *Christ of the Ozarks* statue (1966), sculptor Emmet Sullivan, Eureka Springs, Arkansas. (RosaIreneBetancourt 12/Alamy Stock Photo)

**Figure 47.** *Christ the Redeemer* statue (1922–31), sculptor Paul Landowski, Rio de Janeiro, Brazil. (Gilberto Mesquita / Alamy Stock Photo)

statue to our Savior and for many years we both had longed to see this happen."[3] Smith saw the statue as a bulwark against what he saw as "powerful forces . . . at work to eliminate Christianity from our civilization" and a "standard lifted up in the face of subversion, perversion, atheism, cynicism, materialism, secularism and treason."[4] For some visitors to the *Christ of the Ozarks,* it is a sacred experience to see this homage to Christianity. For others, the statue's awkward aesthetics conjure up the nicknames the "Milk Carton Jesus" and—in a reference to a clay animation figure pervasive in American popular culture—the "Gumby Jesus."

But most visitors to the statue today have little awareness of the statue creator's hate-filled beliefs that profoundly recast its meaning. When Gerald L. K. Smith created the statue after retiring to Eureka Springs with his wife in the 1960s, he attempted to separate the statue from what he glossed over as his "controversial" past. Smith wrote, "It would be sinful and unrefined and un-Christian and un-American for anyone to use such a sacred project to promote any controversial activity."[5] Smith also attempted to obscure his involvement by funding the statue in his wife's name, the Elna M. Smith Foundation. But Smith's past could not be separated from his construction projects on the Eureka Springs mountaintop. A biography of Smith, who was an ordained Disciples of Christ minister and evangelical preacher, named him a "minister of hate." Smith had been deeply involved in American politics since the 1930s, including the Share Our Wealth movement, the Union Party, and the America First Party that espoused far right political views. He founded the Christian National Crusade and ran the publication *Cross and the Flag,* which were both deeply anti-Semitic and racist.[6] Smith believed it was blasphemy to call Jesus a Jew. He used phrases such as "Jewish tyranny," and he denied the Holocaust of World War II had occurred.[7] He believed that the United States was to be "a white, Christian country," and he wrote about black rapists.[8] A *Time* magazine blurb described the *Christ of the Ozarks* statue as not just a Jesus statue but a "snow-white" Jesus statue.[9] This marrying of pure white to Smith's racist views shockingly reshapes how we can and should see the statue. That Smith, who died in 1976 ten years after the statue's dedication, and his wife are buried near the base of the statue, with continuous electronic hymns filling the air nearby as visitors pass by, further recasts the meaning of the statue: the statue is not so much about Jesus as it is about Smith. As the *Time* article put it succinctly, the statue is "a monument to himself."[10]

Most visitors see a statue of Jesus, but the statue is also the oversized grave marker of a man with hate-filled beliefs that contradict the true teachings of Christianity.[11]

## The (Un)Sacred Projects

The *Christ of the Ozarks* statue was just the start of Smith's larger ambition for an evangelical theme park. In 1968 on a second nearby mountaintop, Smith constructed a 3,000-seat amphitheater (later expanded) with elaborate sets of Old Jerusalem for the performance of a Passion play (now called *The Great Passion Play*). Nightly during the summer and fall tourist season, nearly 150 actors from the local community accompanied by a menagerie of sheep, horses, and camels re-create the events of Jesus's condemnation and crucifixion on a 400-foot-long set including Pilate's Court, the Garden of Gethsemane, and Golgotha (fig. 48).[12] Smith also planned to construct a New Holy Land with a replica of the Sea of Galilee and

**Figure 48.** Stage set of *The Great Passion Play*, Eureka Springs, Arkansas. (Photograph by Margaret M. Grubiak)

sets that would "be animated on the order of animated scenes in Disneyland."[13] The Holy Land Tour, as it is now called, is a living history museum where tourists, shuttled on a bus through a reconstructed ancient Middle East landscape entered through a re-creation of Jerusalem's Golden Gate, can interact with actors playing figures in Christ's life and in the culture of Jesus's time (fig. 49).[14] In addition to the Passion play set and Holy Land Tour, Smith also erected the "Christ Only Art Gallery," which today exists as the Sacred Arts Museum, and a Bible Museum. Smith called these constructions his "sacred projects." By 1976, one million people had come to see the Passion play and visit the grounds of Smith's creation.

Gerald L. K. Smith's evangelical theme park—much like Oral Roberts University, Heritage USA, the Creation Museum, and the Ark Encounter—sought to evangelize Christian belief. Yet this evangelical theme park was inescapably tinged with Smith's personal perversion of Christianity. Smith's Passion play was based on one performed in Oberammergau, Germany, since the seventeenth century, which

**Figure 49.** Entrance to the Holy Land Tour, Eureka Springs, Arkansas, through a reconstruction of Jerusalem's Golden Gate. (Photograph by Margaret M. Grubiak)

had a history of foregrounding an anti-Semitic view of Jews' responsibility for the death of Jesus. (Smith even renamed the mountaintop where his Passion play was performed Oberammergau Mountain in an explicit reference to the German play.) Smith created the New Holy Land to provide Christians with a way to experience the world of Jesus without traveling there, but for a hateful reason: he said, "Even the lovers of Christ cannot look upon the birthplace of our Lord without paying cash to a Jew."[15] While ostensibly a celebration of Christianity, Smith's "sacred projects" were driven and shaped by an ideology that condemned Jews in the service of supposedly defending Christ, even as such beliefs disregarded the actual inclusive teachings of Jesus and Christianity.

As these projects were realized in the 1960s, reactions to Gerald L. K. Smith's beliefs espoused in his evangelical theme park ranged from willful ignorance to strident public condemnation. In a story for the *New Yorker* in 1969, Calvin Trillin outlined how the Eureka Springs city council, local business and community leaders, and the local newspaper downplayed Smith's "controversial" beliefs because of the tourism dollars his theme park brought to Eureka Springs, whose heyday in the late nineteenth century as a water cure resort town had faded. But others spoke out against Smith. At the statue's dedication in 1966, Eureka Springs mayor Jan Bullock asserted "that Christ had taught the brotherhood of man and that the statue should be a mecca for all people, regardless of their racial or religious background."[16] The treasurer of the Eureka Springs Chamber of Commerce, "impelled by a deep sense of moral obligation" and concerns that the town would become "so charged with bigotry and racism," quit in protest over the chamber's support of Smith, and letters from others opposing Smith followed her resignation.[17] In 1970, the Jewish Anti-Defamation League of B'nai B'rith called for President Richard Nixon to deny federal funding for a road up to the *Christ of the Ozarks* statue on the grounds that the United States "should not be a partner to a man whose business has been spreading racial and religious bigotry for more than 30 years."[18] Finally, Calvin Trillin reported that, in advance of the Passion play's first performance, the National Council of Catholic Bishops had warned of the misuse of the Passion play for an anti-Semitic agenda.[19] These were strident verbal counters of Smith's views—calls of correction to what some saw as a landscape of hate, not of true religious belief.

Perhaps the most striking visual condemnation of Smith's views as embodied in his "sacred projects" was a threat made but never carried out. According to Smith, the statue had been the subject of multiple bomb threats.[20] Smith may have invented these threats to curry sympathy, for on the face of it the blowing up of a statue of Jesus appeared as an attack on Christianity itself and blasphemy of Christian views. But the threat, had it been carried out, would have been a powerful erasure of Smith's beliefs from the visible landscape. Rather than an act of blasphemy against Christianity, such a visible response—this time of absence—would have been a censure of Smith's own blasphemous marrying of anti-Semitic and racist beliefs to Christianity embodied in the figure of Jesus. Among the responses to landscapes of faith we have encountered in this book, such a threat of violence falls on the extreme end, but it was an (imagined) visible response that was commensurate with the virility of Smith's beliefs.

## Hate's Aesthetic and Historical Neutralization

And yet, today, such protests connecting the landscape of Gerald L. K. Smith's "sacred projects" to his virulent beliefs are themselves absent. Responses to the *Christ of the Ozarks* statue primarily come from aesthetic judgment of the statue's boxy, awkward proportions and "dead eyes." Accounts of the statue's sculptor, Emmet Sullivan, consistently cite that he had previously sculpted dinosaurs for a park in Rapid City, South Dakota, and would go on to create more dinosaur sculptures in Arkansas, a detail that implied Sullivan's artistic abilities were not up to crafting the sacred figure of Christ.[21] The statue has a profound stiffness to it, its body a nearly unarticulated rectangle with only a few skewed lines in slight relief suggesting the draping of robes (see fig. 46). Christ's head is similarly rectangular with an elongated forehead and a severe expression. In 1970, Edgar Albin, a professor in the Department of Art at Southwest Missouri State College and previously at the University of Arkansas in Fayetteville, wrote a scathing review of the statue in the *St. Louis Post-Dispatch*. While Albin acknowledged the racist and anti-Semitic views of Smith, his review focused on a formal, art historical criticism of the statue that he deemed "grossly unsculptural." The statue's outstretched arms were "stuck on without any kind of anatomical orientation," and the "figure and the head are all wrong by any standards of human proportions." Albin quoted a remark by a visitor to the statue that it "looks like a milk carton with a squashed tennis ball on top," a reflection of the nickname "Milk Carton Jesus" that has endured to this day.[22] The statue's other common nickname, "Gumby Jesus," aligns the statue's boxy proportions to the green clay animation figure named Gumby created by filmmaker Art Clokey in the 1950s, whose appearances in television and film have made the figure an American popular culture icon (fig. 50). Because Gumby's blocky shape, suited for clay animation, is

**Figure 50.** Cartoonist Art Clokey with his green clay figure Gumby, which has become a popular culture icon since its creation in the early 1950s. (AP Photo/ Lacy Atkins)

so widely known, the nickname "Gumby Jesus" is an immediately understandable and humorous critique of the *Christ of the Ozarks* statue's awkward form. These humorous nicknames position the statue as roadside curiosity—the *Christ of the Ozarks* is a suggested destination on the website Roadside America—and a piece of religious kitsch, meaning popular and commercialized religious art that does not rise to the level of high art. The statue in this sense of religious kitsch is of a piece with the religious tourism landscape of the Ozarks, including the religious entertainment shows in Branson, Missouri; Samuel Butcher's Precious Moments Chapel in Carthage, Missouri, which places the popular religious memento sculptures Precious Moments in a re-created version of the Sistine Chapel; and Jim Bakker's reincarnated theme park Morningside in Blue Eye, Missouri.[23]

Yet this framing of the *Christ of the Ozarks* statue as religious kitsch and an aesthetic failure obscures and neutralizes the corrosive history of hate that was endemic to the landscape Gerald L. K. Smith created. Art critic Edgar Albin was prophetic in his assertion in 1970 that "time will perhaps have eradicated some of the details of how the statue came about" and that Smith's "anti-Semitic and racist publications may, too, have been forgotten by then." Albin recounted, and judged, what remains a common experience of visitors to the statue:

The "Christ of the Ozarks" succeeds in symbolizing to mass man his sentimental values. Tourists silently tread the flinty path to the hill and once there, with funeral home hymns being amplified at rock and roll volume around them on scratchy tape, they speak in hushed tones as if they were in some great cathedral. There is nothing sacred, nothing consecrated, nothing hallowed about this land on top of Magnetic Mountain, yet the symbol strikes the tourist with awe and he is blind to its ugliness and sham.[24]

Albin's criticism, though scathing and condescending, makes plain the differing reactions to Gerald L. K. Smith's landscape of faith and the complexity of our reactions over time. For those who remember Smith's racism and anti-Semitism, the statue, the Passion play, and the New Holy Land were far from "sacred projects" but rather a perversion of the true teachings of Christ and another vehicle for Smith to make money for his other hate-filled enterprises. For these people, Smith's landscape is paradoxically a landscape of Smith's own doubt, his own blindness to what Jesus taught. But for others who do not know or remember Smith's views, the reaction is very different. Those who call it the "Milk Carton Jesus" and "Gumby Jesus" may be aware of its "ugliness" in a formal sense but not the weightier sense of the perversion or "sham" of Christian theology that Albin intended. And for those visitors simply wanting to see a monument to Christ and Christianity, the reaction to it can be an experience of sacred space and object. They can feel reverence and closeness to Christ in our world and time.

The *Christ of the Ozark* statue is a microcosm of the complex interplay between faith and doubt prompted in our built environment. It raises questions about the human construction of religious landscapes—what Smith intended (Was it a monument to Jesus, or a monument to himself?) and what was unintended (How do we understand the "Milk Carton Jesus" and "Gumby Jesus" monikers that critique the statue's artistic value within a popular culture frame?). This landscape of faith raises questions about institutional religion (How do we reconcile Smith's views about Jews and African Americans with his claims to Christian membership and his identity as an ordained Disciples of Christ minister?) as well as particular questions about theology (What is the relationship between Christianity and Judaism? How might we view ecumenical relationships across religions that have differing views on the figures of salvation?). More troubling, this landscape of faith and doubt asks whether visitors are unwittingly complicit in Smith's perversion of Christian beliefs in their consumption of this evangelical theme park. While presented as a landscape of faith, the *Christ of the Ozarks* statue and its "sacred projects" are also a landscape of doubt—of Smith's own doubts of Jesus's teachings and a larger public's doubts about the perversion of religion. And it is a landscape of faith and doubt that has changed, and continues to change, with time and memory.

# CONCLUSION

Landscapes of doubt are born of landscapes of faith. They are cut from the same cloth, though they operate in different ways. Where landscapes of faith assert, landscapes of doubt respond. Where landscapes of faith are sincere, landscapes of doubt are irreverent, even sacrilegious. Where landscapes of faith focus our attention on those insiders who adhere to belief and practice it, landscapes of doubt focus our attention on those outsiders, and sometimes insiders, who use their freedom from the strictures of faith to recast religious meaning, challenging it and raising questions. The enduring power of landscapes of faith and doubt is awakening us to these fundamental questions of faith in ways we may not otherwise seek out.

These questions of faith fall in two categories. First, landscapes of faith and doubt generate questions about the human construction of religion and institutional religion, including Christianity, which has been the focus of this book. "Touchdown Jesus" at the University of Notre Dame asks us: If we think of sports as a religion, does that dilute or undermine religion as traditionally understood? The Mormon Washington D.C. Temple as *The Wizard of Oz* asks us: How do we understand The Church of Jesus Christ of Latter-day Saints, founded in America in the nineteenth century, relative to Christian denominations that have a longer history? Did Joseph Smith invent a religion out of thin air, or are all religions created in this manner? The evangelical theme park at Heritage USA and Oral Roberts University asks us: Are televangelists exemplars of the prosperity gospel, or are they religious hucksters scamming vulnerable people out of money? How do we see the motives of the people who help to shape our spiritual lives in organized religion? The Creation Museum and Ark Encounter ask us: How do we deal with fundamentalist religions that have little compromise for those who stand outside of their beliefs? How do we hold beliefs that counter the beliefs of others, and still live in community with them? And "Gumby Jesus" asks us: Can we separate those who claim Christian membership while holding hate-filled beliefs from the theology of Christianity itself?

Second, landscapes of faith and doubt generate questions about the substance of faith itself. Are God and Jesus present in our world and our time, or are they are constructs of a distant time and place? How should we pray, and to what end? Can we direct God's will with prayer, and even manipulate outcomes to what we desire? Where did religious texts such as the Bible and the Book of Mormon come from, and are they the word of God? Are religious visions real? Can we be healed by faith alone? Who created humans and the world, and how? What do we believe about the next world, the one we may see after our deaths? How do we reconcile our fallible humanity to a moral way of life?

Landscapes of faith and doubt ask us, adamantly, to contemplate, weigh, refine, and ultimately clarify what it is we believe. They engage us in ways that are different from a Sunday sermon or a scripture reading—in ways more accessible, more intelligible, and more entertaining. Drawing on humor, satire, sacrilege, and popular culture, landscapes of doubt put us in conversation with landscapes of faith to create a richer, more illuminating account of what we believe. This questioning of religion is the unintended construction of meaning that Dell Upton described for us. Landscapes of faith and doubt underscore that religion is deeply part of our cultural landscapes, where these fundamental questions about faith are not limited solely to the Sabbath, or solely to those priests, pastors, rabbis, and theologians who are the keepers of official religious dogma, or solely to the walls of church and temple. Landscapes of faith and doubt make the most important questions—about what we believe, about how we live our lives, about what we think the purpose of our life is—real, alive, and pressing to our everyday, lived experience.

# NOTES

INTRODUCTION

1. Oral Roberts, "I Must Tell Somebody . . . And I Must Tell You, Dear Partner . . . ," *Abundant Life* (Tulsa, OK) 24, no. 8 (September 1980): 10.

2. As quoted in Harrell, *Oral Roberts,* 415. For other accounts of Roberts's vision, see "Oral Roberts Tells of Talking to 900-Foot Jesus," *Tulsa World,* October 16, 1980; and Robert L. Dorman, *It Happened in Oklahoma: Remarkable Events That Shaped History* (Guildford, CT: Globe Pequot Press, 2012), 124–28. While Roberts had the vision in May 1980 as construction of the towers was underway, he did not reveal his vision until months later in September 1980 in an appeal to his prayer partners to bring to life what Jesus had foreseen and promised.

3. For this image, see Roberts, "I Must Tell Somebody," 11.

4. Harrell, *Oral Roberts,* 415–16.

5. Harrell, *Oral Roberts,* 417.

6. Harrell, *Oral Roberts,* 416, 597n174.

7. Robert McAfee Brown, "Oral Roberts and the 900-Foot Jesus: Investigating the Credibility of a Claim from the Oral Tradition," *Christian Century,* April 22, 1981, 450–52; reprinted in William H. Willimon, *And the Laugh Shall Be First: A Treasury of Religious Humor* (Nashville: Abingdon Press, 1986), 148–56.

8. For the story of the genesis of this name, see Chris Heim, "An Encounter with MC 900 Ft. Jesus," *Chicago Tribune,* April 13, 1990, 161.

9. "A Cross to Bear," *Saturday Oklahoman and Times* (Oklahoma City), December 19, 1981, 19.

10. Upton, "Architectural History," 197. Emphasis in the original.

11. Upton, "Architectural History, 198.

12. For an understanding of religion within culture, see Geertz, "Religion as a Cultural System." For concepts of popular religion or lived religion—the encountering of religion in the everyday—see Williams, *Popular Religion in America;* Lippy, *Being Religious;* and Orsi, "Everyday Miracles."

13. See Morgan and Promey, *Visual Culture;* Morgan, *Religion and Material Culture;* McDannell, *Material Christianity;* and Gretchen Buggeln, *The Suburban Church: Modernism and Community in Postwar America* (Minneapolis: University of Minnesota Press, 2016).

14. Morgan, *Sacred Gaze,* 6.

15. McDannell, *Material Christianity,* 2. Emphasis in the original.

16. Cristina Garduño Freeman, "Participatory Culture as a Site for the Reception of Architecture: Making a Giant Sydney Opera House Cake," *Architectural Theory Review* 18, no. 3 (2013): 334.

17. For overview discussions of religion and popular culture, see Albanese, "Religion and Popular Culture"; Mazur and McCarthy, "Introduction: Finding Religion in American Popular Culture," *God in the Details,* 1–15; and Bruce David Forbes, "Introduction: Finding Religion in Unexpected Places," in Forbes and Mahan, *Religion and Popular Culture,* 1–20.

18. Erika Doss, *Elvis Culture: Fans, Faith, and Image* (Lawrence: University Press of Kansas, 1999); Kathryn Lofton, *Oprah: The Gospel of an Icon* (Berkeley: University of California Press, 2011); Novak, *Joy of Sports;* Chidester, *Authentic Fakes.* See also Rodash, *Rapture Ready!;* and Feltmate, *Drawn to the Gods.*

19. "Heritage USA," Wikipedia.org, https://en.wikipedia.org/wiki/Heritage_USA.

20. Beatriz Colomina, *Privacy and Publicity: Modern Architecture as Mass Media* (Cambridge, MA: MIT Press, 1994).

21. Naomi Stead and Cristina Garduño Freeman, "Architecture and 'The Act of Receiving, or the Fact of Being Received,'" *Architectural Theory Review* 18, no. 3 (2013): 269.

22. For overview histories of religious satire, see Lindvall, *God Mocks;* and Kantra, *All Things Vain.* For the role of religious humor as opposed to satire in the "inner dialectic of the sacred and the comic," see Hyers, *Holy Laughter.* See also Feltmate, "It's Funny"; and Feltmate, "Religion and Humor." Feltmate offers a reassessment of religion and humor in Peter Berger's well-known work, *Redeeming Laughter.* David Chidester gives a case study of religion and humor based on

incongruity in South Africa in *Religion: Material Dynamics* (Oakland: University of California Press, 2018), 58–72; I am grateful to Gretchen Buggeln for calling my attention to this work.

23. Plate, *Blasphemy,* 34; and Morgan, *Sacred Gaze,* 115–46. See also Francois Boespflug, "Laughing at God: The Pictorial History of Boundaries Not to Be Crossed," in *Humour and Religion: Challenges and Ambiguities,* ed. Hans Geybels and Walter Van Herck (London: Continuum International, 2011), 204–17.

24. See Nelson Goodman, "How Buildings Mean," *Critical Inquiry* 11, no. 4 (June 1985): 642–53.

25. For another understanding of religious insiders and outsiders, see Moore, *Religious Outsiders.*

26. As quoted in Schmitt, *Words of Life,* 72.

27. John Laing, as quoted in Kent Larsen, "In View of Temple, Graffiti Again Seeks Dorothy's Surrender," *Mormon News,* December 3, 2001, http://www.mormonstoday.com/011207/D1WashDCTemple01.shtml.

28. For works that do engage these ideas, though not necessarily in regard to religious architecture and image, see Courtney Bender and Pamela Klassen, eds. *After Pluralism: Reimagining Religious Engagement* (New York: Columbia University Press, 2010); Judith Butler, Jurgen Habermas, Charles Taylor, and Cornel West, *The Power of Religion in the Public Sphere* (New York: Columbia University Press, 2011); Jose Casanova, *Public Religions in the Modern World* (Chicago: University of Chicago Press, 1994); Peter Gottschalk, *American Heretics: Catholic, Jews, Muslims, and the History of Religious Intolerance* (New York: Palgrave Macmillan, 2013); William Hutchinson, *Religious Pluralism in America: The Contentious History of a Founding Ideal* (New Haven, CT: Yale University Press, 2003); Barbara A. McGraw and Jo Renee Formicola, eds., *Taking Religious Pluralism Seriously: Spiritual Politics on America's Sacred Ground* (Waco, TX: Baylor University Press, 2005); Sally M. Promey, "The Public Display of Religion," in Morgan and Promey, *Visual Culture,* 27–48; Stephen Prothero, *Religious Literacy: What Every American Needs to Know—and Doesn't* (New York: HarperCollins, 2007); and Isaac Weiner, *Religion Out Loud: Religious Sound, Public Space, and American Pluralism* (New York: New York University Press, 2014).

29. For a story of an encountering of belief in the American landscape through roadside religious attractions that also remakes personal belief, see Beal, *Roadside Religion.*

1. TOUCHDOWN JESUS!

1. Scott Eden, *Touchdown Jesus: Faith and Fandom at Notre Dame* (New York: Simon & Schuster, 2005).

2. Moore, *Touchdown Jesus,* 11.

3. For critical histories of the Hesburgh Library, see the well-researched account by Marsha Stevenson, "Style and Symbol: Library Buildings at Notre Dame," in *What Is Written Remains: Historical Essays on the Libraries of Notre Dame,* ed. Maureen Gleason and Katharina J. Blackstead (Notre Dame, IN: University of Notre Dame Press, 1994) and Schmitt, *Words of Life.*

4. On the separation of American universities from their founding religious dominations, see James Tunstead Burtchaell, *The Dying of the Light: The Disengagement of Colleges and Universities from Their Christian Churches* (Grand Rapids, MI: W. B. Eerdmans, 1998); George M. Marsden, *The Soul of the American University: From Protestant Establishment to Established Nonbelief* (New York: Oxford University Press, 1994); and Jon H. Roberts and James Turner, *The Sacred and the Secular University* (Princeton, NJ: Princeton University Press, 2000). For an excellent case study of this phenomenon, see P. C. Kemeny, *Princeton in the Nation's Service: Religious Ideals and Educational Practice, 1868–1928* (New York: Oxford University Press, 1998). For the architectural consequences of this separation, see Grubiak, *White Elephants on Campus.*

5. University of Notre Dame and NewGroupMedia, "Word of Life Mural: Touchdown Jesus," video, 6:06 minutes, 2003, posted on YouTube August 29, 2013, https://youtu.be/vtw QryxwVx8, accessed November 30, 2017.

6. On the early uses of the term "Touchdown Jesus," see Schmitt, *Words of Life,* 72–75.

7. Higgs, *God in the Stadium,* 287.

8. See Joseph L. Price, "The Pitcher's Mound as Cosmic Mountain: The Religious Significance of Baseball," in Price, *From Season to Season,* 61–76.

9. Novak, *Joy of Sports,* 31, 21, as quoted in Joseph L. Price, "An American Apotheosis: Sports as Popular Religion," in Price, *From Season to Season,* 223.

10. Price, "American Apotheosis," 229.

11. Novak, *Joy of Sports,* 21; Price, "American Apotheosis," 229.

12. Novak, *Joy of Sports,* 21; Price, "American Apotheosis," 220.

13. Novak, *Joy of Sports,* 21; Price, "American Apotheosis," 229.

14. Novak, *Joy of Sports,* 21.

15. Price, "American Apotheosis," 229.

16. Scholes and Sassower, *Religion and Sports,* 11.

17. Price, "American Apotheosis," 217; Scholes and Sassower, *Religion and Sports,* 19. Emphasis in the original.

18. David Morgan, "Emotion and Imagination in the Ritual Entanglement of Religion, Sport, and Nationalism," in *Feeling Religion,* ed. John Corrigan (Durham, NC: Duke University Press, 2017), 230.

19. As quoted in Schmitt, *Words of Life,* 70.

20. Joseph L. Price, "From Sabbath Proscriptions to Super Sunday Celebrations: Sports and Religion in America," in Price, *From Season to Season,* 34.

21. Baker, *Playing with God,* 129.

22. Thomas J. Schlereth, *The University of Notre Dame: A Portrait of Its History and Campus* (Notre Dame, IN: University of Notre Dame Press, 1976), 210. See Sandra Dipasqua and Barbara Calamari, *Holy Cards* (New York: Harry N. Abrams, 2004).

23. Schmitt, *Words of Life,* 154.

24. Ed Sherman, "Holtz's Logic on God's Role More Holey than Holy," *Chicago Tribune,* North Sports Final, C ed., September 27, 1990, 1, as referenced in Hoffman, *Good Game,* 248; and Price, "From Sabbath Proscriptions," 31.

25. As quoted in Price, "From Sabbath Proscriptions," 31.

26. Price, "From Sabbath Proscriptions," 31.

27. As quoted in William Nack, "Does God Care Who Wins the Super Bowl?," *Sports Illustrated,* January 26, 1998, 8.

28. As quoted in Nack, "Does God Care," 47.

29. As quoted in Sherman, "Holtz's Logic," 1.

30. Hoffman, *Good Game,* 244. For how Christian prayer operates in sports, see Hoffman, *Good Game,* 239–62.

31. Hoffman, *Good Game,* 252.

32. Price, "From Sabbath Proscriptions," 18–19.

33. On Christians and sports and the concept of "sportaniety," see Hoffman, *Good Game,* 1–22.

34. See Kevin Lixey, "The Vatican's Game Plan for Maximizing Sport's Educational Potential," in *Sports and Christianity: Historical and Contemporary Perspectives,* ed. Nick J. Watson and Andrew Parker (New York: Routledge, 2013), 250–68.

35. Julie Bryne, *O God of Players: The Story of the Immaculata Mighty Macs* (New York: Columbia University Press, 2003).

36. See Alexander Leitch, "The Christian Student," in *A Princeton Companion* (Princeton, NJ: Princeton University Press, 1978), 96–97 and Kemeny, *Princeton in the Nation's Service,* 187, 216.

37. For a discussion of this transformation, see Clotfelter, *Big-Time Sports.*

38. Clotfelter, *Big-Time Sports,* 18.

39. Charles Clotfelter's main argument is that universities are indeed in "the entertainment business." For an overview of his argument, see *Big-Time Sports,* 3–22.

40. Higgs, *God in the Stadium,* 285.

41. For a discussion of scholars who do not see sports as fully a religion, see Price, "American Apotheosis," 217.

42. Eire, *War against the Idols*, 2.

43. Eire, *War against the Idols*, 1.

44. Eire, *War against the Idols*, 2, 3.

45. For further discussion on the visual culture of Protestantism, see Morgan, introduction to *Icons of American Protestantism*, 4–18.

46. John Davis, "Catholic Envy: The Visual Culture of Protestant Desire," in Morgan and Promey, *Visual Culture*, 108–9.

47. David Morgan, "Warner Sallman and the Visual Culture of American Protestantism," in Morgan, *Icons of American Protestantism*, 26.

48. Smith, *Story of the Statue*, 5–6.

49. Hofstadter, *Anti-Intellectualism*, 140, 139. A parallel claim about anti-intellectualism among American evangelicals in the late twentieth century was made by Noll, *Scandal*.

50. Hofstadter, *Anti-Intellectualism*, 139.

51. Monsignor John Tracy Ellis, "American Catholics and the Intellectual Life," *Thought* 30 (Autumn 1955): 351–88.

52. Alice Gallin, O.S.U., *Negotiating Identity: Catholic Higher Education since 1960* (Notre Dame, IN: University of Notre Dame Press, 2000), 3.

53. Quoted in John H. Janowski, ed., "Notre Dame Memorial Library Dedication," *Notre Dame* 17, no. 2 (1964): 2.

54. Thomas J. Fleming, "Hesburgh of Notre Dame — (1) 'He's Destroying the University' (2) 'He's Bringing It into the Mainstream of American Life,'" *New York Times Sunday Magazine*, May 11, 1969, 64.

55. Fleming, "Hesburgh of Notre Dame," 64.

56. Fleming, "Hesburgh of Notre Dame," 59–60.

57. Fleming, "Hesburgh of Notre Dame," 60.

58. For a discussion of the perception of Catholic intellectual weakness, see Philip Gleason, *Contending with Modernity: Catholic Higher Education in the Twentieth Century* (New York: Oxford University Press, 1995), 287–96.

59. A well-known example of Hesburgh's support of academic freedom in the 1950s was the defense of the Reverend John Courtney Murray, S.J., who came under attack by the Vatican for a paper he gave at Notre Dame on academic freedom, which Notre Dame later published. In 1967 at a meeting of the North American region of the International Federation of Catholic Universities, Hesburgh helped draft the "Statement on the Nature of the Contemporary Catholic University," which asserted, "The whole world of knowledge and ideas must be open

to the students; there must be no outlawed books or subjects." In recognition of Hesburgh's commitment to academic freedom, the American Association of University Professors awarded Hesburgh the Alexander Meiklejohn Award for Academic Freedom in 1970. For Hesburgh's position on academic freedom, see Theodore M. Hesburgh, C.S.C., with Jerry Reedy, *God, Country, Notre Dame: The Autobiography of Theodore M. Hesburgh* (New York: Doubleday, 1990), 223–45.

60. Theodore M. Hesburgh, C.S.C., *The Hesburgh Papers: Higher Values in Higher Education* (Kansas City, KS: Andrews and McMeel, 1979), 64.

61. Hesburgh quoted in "God and Man at Notre Dame," *Time,* February 9, 1962, 54.

62. Following the "Program for the Future," the Challenge II (1963–66) and SUMMA (1967–72) campaigns raised a combined $80 million for capital projects as well as academic programs, institutes, and scholarships. See Schlereth, *University of Notre Dame,* 208–9.

63. The $6 million was a matching grant for $12 million, which Notre Dame surpassed in its collection of $18 million. The Ford Foundation also awarded grants to Vanderbilt University and the University of Denver, making the University of Notre Dame the only Catholic institution selected for the award.

64. University of Notre Dame press release, September 25, 1960, Information Services 18/10a, University Archives, University of Notre Dame, Notre Dame, IN.

65. John N. Cackley Jr., ed. *Notre Dame Memorial Library* (Notre Dame, IN: University of Notre Dame, 1960), 3, found in PNDP 10-He-1, University Archives, University of Notre Dame, Notre Dame, IN.

66. Cackley, *Notre Dame Memorial Library,* 10.

67. Victor A. Schaefer to Reverend Philip S. Moore, May 6, 1959, UODL 33/44, University Archives, University of Notre Dame, Notre Dame, IN.

68. Victor A. Schaefer, "Notre Dame's Mosaic Tower," *Library Journal* 89 (1964): 4743.

69. For a history of modernism within American Catholic buildings, see Osborne, *American Catholics.*

70. Schlereth, *University of Notre Dame,* 210.

71. University of Notre Dame, *The Word of Life* (Notre Dame, IN: University of Notre Dame, University Libraries, 2004), found in PDNP 10-He-2, University Archives, University of Notre Dame, Notre Dame, IN.

72. Hesburgh, quoted in University of Notre Dame, *Word of Life.* On occasion of his visit to UNAM, Father Hesburgh received a certificate from the university on April 18, 1955. See Theodore M. Hesburgh Papers (OPHS), Box 6, University Archives, University of Notre Dame, Notre Dame, IN. Hesburgh also noted that the library and its murals in Caracas, Venezuela, had also been an inspiration.

73. Jack Rowe, "Behind the Mural," *Notre Dame Scholastic* 105, no. 21 (1964): 31. Phalin here is referring to UNAM.

74. Father Theodore M. Hesburgh, interview with the author, July 15, 2009.

75. Valerie Fraser, *Building the New World: Studies in the Modern Architecture of Latin America, 1930–1960* (London: Verso, 2000), 62.

76. "World's Fanciest Campus," *Time,* February 23, 1953. See also Esther McCoy, "Cuidad Universitaria de Mexico," *Northwest Architect* 16, no. 5 (1952): 4–8, 24–30, 42. I am grateful to Edward Burian and Keith Eggener for suggesting sources on Juan O'Gorman and the UNAM campus.

77. Celia Ester Arredondo Zambrano, "Modernity in Mexico: The Case of the Cuidad Universitaria," in *Modernity and the Architecture of Mexico,* ed. Edward R. Burian (Austin: University of Texas Press, 1997), 91–106.

78. Juan O'Gorman, *La Palabra de Juan O'Gorman (Selección de textos),* ed. Ida Rodríguez Prampolini, Olga Sáenz, and Elizabeth Fuentes Rojas (Mexico City: Universidad Nacional Autónoma de México, 1983), 297. Translated from the Spanish.

79. On the UNAM library's murals, see also Kathryn E. O'Rourke, *Modern Architecture in Mexico City: History, Representation, and the Shaping of a Capital* (Pittsburgh: University of Pittsburgh Press, 2016), 251–58.

80. O'Gorman, *La Palabra de Juan O'Gorman,* 296.

81. O'Gorman, *La Palabra de Juan O'Gorman,* 297.

82. O'Gorman, *La Palabra de Juan O'Gorman,* 297.

83. Many scholars have observed this symbolism within the murals. For example, see Juan Manuel Heredia, "Transparency of an Opaque Surface: Juan O'Gorman's Central Library at the University of Mexico," *On Site Review* 9 (2003): 34; Fraser, *Building the New World,* 81; and O'Rourke, *Modern Architecture,* 253.

84. Transcript of interview between Millard Sheets and Father John H. Wilson, ca. May 1964, Notre Dame Printed & Reference Material Dropfiles (PNDP) 10-He-2, University Archives, University of Notre Dame, Notre Dame, IN. As Sheets stated in this interview, this mural's angularity was determined in large part by the granite materials: "in dealing with the inflexibility of granite it is better to deal with it and work with it rather than fight it."

85. Frederic Whitaker, "Millard Sheets, The Story of a Giant," *American Artist* 28 (1964): 34.

86. Transcript of interview between Millard Sheets and Father John H. Wilson, ca. May 1964, Notre Dame Printed & Reference Material Dropfiles (PNDP) 10-He-2, University Archives, University of Notre Dame, Notre Dame, IN.

87. As quoted in Schmitt, *Words of Life,* 70.

88. University of Notre Dame, *Word of Life.*

89. University of Notre Dame and NewGroupMedia, "Word of Life Mural."

## 2. DOROTHY, *THE WIZARD OF OZ,* AND THE MORMON TEMPLE

1. These defensive forms have a long history in Mormon architecture. As Terryl L. Givens notes, early Mormon temples in the nineteenth century in Utah are described as being "militant, defiant, or imperial." See Givens, *People of Paradox,* 246. For a detailed history of Mormon material culture in the nineteenth century, see Carter, *Building Zion.*

2. Taylor Branch, "Castle of Refuge: The Mormon's Bunker against Apocalypse," *Harper's Weekly,* November 22, 1974, 5; Chip Brown, "The Mysterious Citadel on the Beltway," *Washington Post,* May 24, 1981, A1, A16–A17.

3. As quoted in "Behind the Temple Walls," *Time,* September 16, 1974, 110.

4. "Wicked Witch of the Beltway?," *Montgomery Journal* (Chevy Chase, MD), October 31, 1974. See especially the accompanying photograph by Hoke Kempley. See also John Kelly, "Search for 'Surrender Dorothy' Scrawler Pulls Back Curtain on Schoolgirl Prank," *Washington Post,* July 22, 2011, for a recounting of the story and a reproduction of the Kempley image.

5. For a history of the graffiti, see Michael de Groote, "D.C. Temple Prank Won't Die," *Deseret News* (Salt Lake City), July 26, 2011. For more recent graffiti incursions on the bridge, see, for example, Bethany Rodgers, "Message 'Surrender Donald' Appears on Beltway Overpass Near Mormon Temple," *Bethesda Magazine,* August 24, 2018.

6. "Surrender, Dorothy!," *The Wizard of Oz,* 70th anniversary ed., directed by Victor Fleming (1939; Burbank, CA: Warner Home Video, 2009), DVD.

7. Although The Church of Jesus Christ of Latter-day Saints (LDS) is a specific denomination within a broader category of Mormonism, I use "Mormon" and "Mormonism" in this chapter to mean the LDS Church.

8. Wilcox, *Washington DC Temple,* n.p.

9. "Mormons Unveil a Striking Monument," *U.S. News and World Report,* September 23, 1974, 56.

10. Wilcox, *Washington DC Temple,* n.p.

11. Klaus D. Gurgel, *The 1974 Washington Temple Survey: A Socio-spatial Analysis* (Syracuse University, 1975), 1.

12. Sally M. Promey, "The Public Display of Religion" in Morgan and Promey, *Visual Culture,* 38.

13. Promey, "Public Display of Religion," 38, 39.

14. As quoted in Haws, *Mormon Image, 77.*

15. Haws, *Mormon Image, 78.*

16. See Haws, *Mormon Image,* chapter 3, "Church Rites versus Civil Rights," 47–73, for a discussion of the controversy over blacks as priesthood holders, and 86–95, for a discussion on the Mormon stance on the Equal Rights Amendment.

17. For Mormons' influence in American popular culture in the 1970s and in other eras, see J. Michael Hunter, ed., *Mormons and Popular Culture: The Global Influence of an American Phenomenon,* vols. 1–2 (Santa Barbara, CA: Praeger, 2013).

18. Hawes, *Mormon Image,* 75–81.

19. Stephen W. Stathis and Dennis L. Lythgoe, "Mormonism in the Nineteen-Seventies: The Popular Perception," *Dialogue: A Journal of Mormon Thought* 10, no. 3 (Spring 1977): 111.

20. While the New York World's Fair was the first fair at which the Mormons specifically constructed a pavilion, the Mormons had a presence at previous world's fairs, including the 1893 World's Columbian Exposition. For an account of this early experience, see Reid L. Neilson, *Exhibiting Mormonism: The Latter-day Saints and the 1893 Chicago World's Fair* (New York: Oxford University Press, 2011).

21. Nathaniel Smith Kogan argues "the more durable and distinctive legacy of the Mormon Pavilion lies in the role it played in creating a corporate image for the LDS Church and in systematically communicating that identity to a variety of audiences in future pavilions and visitors' centers." See Nathaniel Smith Kogan, "Mormons in the New York World's Fair, 1964–1965," in Hunter, *Mormons and Popular Culture,* 218.

22. Julie Nicoletta, "Selling Spirituality and Spectacle: Religious Pavilions at the New York World's Fair of 1964–65," *Buildings & Landscapes: Journal of the Vernacular Architecture Forum* 22, no. 2 (Fall 2015): 78.

23. For a history of the Mormon Pavilion at the 1964 fair, see also Kogan, "Mormons in the New York World's Fair," 209–23; Brent L. Top, "Legacy of the Mormon Pavilion," *Ensign,* October 1989, 22–23; and Taylor Petrey, "New York 1964 World's Fair: Mormonism's Global Introduction," *New York LDS Historian* 3, no. 2 (Fall 2000): 1–2, 4, 6, 8–11.

24. Gurgel, *1974 Washington Temple Survey,* 19, 21, 23.

25. Gurgel, *1974 Washington Temple Survey,* 72.

26. Gurgel, *1974 Washington Temple Survey,* 74, 76.

27. As quoted in Gurgel, *1974 Washington Temple Survey ,* 70.

28. Wilcox, *Washington DC Temple,* n.p.

29. As quoted in C. Brown, "Mysterious Citadel," A16.

30. Gurgel, *1974 Washington Temple Survey,* 7.

31. For accounts by those who toured the temple in 1974, see "Behind the Temple Walls,"

110–11; Forshey, "The Scholars and the Washington Temple," *Christian Century,* January 15, 1975, 30–31; Paul Goldberger, "New Mormon Temple: $15-Million Conversation Piece," *New York Times,* November 12, 1974, 30; and "Washington Monument," *Newsweek,* September 9, 1974, 72.

32. Goldberger, "New Mormon Temple," 30.

33. C. Brown, "Mysterious Citadel," A16. For an extended analysis of the Washington D.C. Temple as a Space Age structure, see Steven Cornell, "Space, Race, and Symbol: The Rocket Ship on the Beltway," *Utah-rchitecture* (blog), March 17, 2010, http://utah-rchitecture.blogspot .com/2010/03/space-race-and-symbol-rocket-ship-on.html.

34. Goldberger, "New Mormon Temple," 30.

35. Forshey, "Scholars and the Washington Temple," 30–31.

36. "Behind the Temple Walls," 110; Goldberger, "New Mormon Temple," 30. Goldberger here is referring to Forest Lawn Cemetery in Los Angeles, renowned for its celebrity inhabitants and miniaturized architectural monuments, considered by some as tacky.

37. Goldberger, "New Mormon Temple," 30.

38. While published descriptions about the nature of these rites exist, a veil of secrecy nevertheless persists about their actual content, even to Latter-day Saints who may never enter a temple in their lifetime. For a description by The Church of Jesus Christ of Latter-day Saints of the religious rites that take place in the Washington DC Temple, see Spencer W. Kimball, *Welcome to Our Temple* (Salt Lake City [?]: The Church of Jesus Christ of Latter-day Saints, 1974). For an updated, public description of these rites by The Church of Jesus Christ of Latter-day Saints, see "About the Temple Endowment," https://www.lds.org/temples/what -is-temple-endowment?. For an outsider description of these rites, see Leone, "New Mormon Temple," 51.

39. Anthropologist Mark Leone, who toured the Washington D.C. Temple during the public open house, wrote an analysis of the temple in which he argued that the temple's layout is a realization of the Mormon emphasis on the family unit and the self. The circulation pattern of the building—its many corridors, stairs, and elevators—makes it possible in this huge building, serving hundreds of thousands of Mormons in the course of a year, to experience it individually or within small groups. To support this claim, Leone also pointed to the building's beehive references, a metaphor for the individual within the community invoked throughout the history of Mormonism, which is inscribed in the temple's hexagonal shape. Leone argued the atomization of space in a Mormon temple reflects the compartmentalization that Mormons must make in their minds to both reconcile with and protect their worldview from a majority American culture that is at odds with Mormon belief, though some scholars such as Colleen McDannell reject this interpretation. See Leone, "New Mormon Temple," 46–47, 53.

40. Wilcox, *Washington DC Temple,* n.p. These "nationally known architects" remain unidentified.

41. Wilcox, *Washington DC Temple,* n.p.

42. For a description of New Formalism or Modern Classicism, see Dale Allen Gyure, *Minoru Yamasaki: Humanistic Architecture for a Modernist World* (New Haven, CT: Yale University Press, 2017), 126–27.

43. Douglas Haskell, "Architecture and Popular Taste," *Architectural Forum* 109 (August 1958): 104–9. For a contextual introduction to the importance of Haskell's article, see Gabrielle Esperdy, "Architecture and Popular Taste," *Places Journal,* May 2015, https://doi.org/10.22269/150504.

44. Haskell, "Architecture and Popular Taste," 104–9.

45. Goldberger, "New Mormon Temple," 30. For the gendered and pejorative naming of this kind of architecture as the "Ballet School," coined by Reyner Banham, see Gyure, *Minoru Yamasaki,* 154–57.

46. See Charles A. Jencks, *The Language of Post-Modern Architecture* (New York: Rizzoli, 1977), and Robert Venturi, Denise Scott Brown, and Steven Izenour, *Learning from Las Vegas* (Cambridge, MA: MIT Press, 1972).

47. Goldberger, "New Mormon Temple," 30.

48. For interpretations of how Americans see *The Wizard of Oz* in a common culture, see Paul Nathanson, *Over the Rainbow:* The Wizard of Oz *as a Secular Myth of America* (Albany: State University of New York Press, 1991). For other understandings of allegories of Oz, see Henry Littlefield's well-known exploration of the story as a commentary on American populism in Henry M. Littlefield, "*The Wizard of Oz:* Parable on Populism," *American Quarterly* 16, no. 1 (Spring 1964): 47–58; and Ranjit Dighe, ed., *The Historian's* Wizard of Oz: *Reading L. Frank Baum's Classic as a Political and Monetary Allegory* (Westport, CT: Praeger, 2002).

49. See Eliade, *Sacred and the Profane,* 36–47.

50. Wilcox, *Washington DC Temple,* n.p.

51. On the Latter-day Saints building of Zion, see Carter, *Building Zion.* For a history of Zion as a concept, see Martin Buber, *On Zion: The History of an Idea* (New York: Schocken Books, 1973).

52. For Oz as sacred space, see Richard Tuerk, *Oz in Perspective: Magic and Myth in the L. Frank Baum Books* (Jefferson, NC: McFarland), 178–90.

53. "Behind the Temple Walls," 110.

54. As quoted in C. Brown, "Mysterious Citadel on the Beltway," A16.

55. Leone, "New Mormon Temple," 58.

56. As quoted in Tuerk, *Oz in Perspective,* 36–37.

57. As quoted in Tuerk, *Oz in Perspective,* 161.

58. As quoted in J. Spencer Fluhman, *"A Peculiar People": Anti-Mormonism and the Making of Religion in Nineteenth-Century America* (Chapel Hill: University of North Carolina Press, 2012), 21.

59. Tuerk, *Oz in Perspective,* 37–40.

60. Fluhman, *"Peculiar People,"* 10–11. For an understanding of Mormonism in the nineteenth century, see also Shipps, *Mormonism.*

61. For an extensive analysis of Mormon garments, see McDannell, *Material Christianity,* 198–221.

62. de Groote, "D.C. Temple Prank Won't Die"; "Temple's Soaring Spires Called Sight for Sore Eyes," *Deseret News* (Salt Lake City), May 23, 1989.

63. John Laing, as quoted in Larsen, "In View of Temple."

64. I am grateful to Emily Utt, Historic Sites curator, LDS Church History Department, for providing this earlier history of LDS Bureaus of Information, which were renamed "Visitors' Centers" in the 1960s.

## 3. ADVENTURES IN THE EVANGELICAL THEME PARK

1. With origins on *The Tracey Ullman Show* in 1987, *The Simpsons* began airing its half-hour format in December 1989—the episode in which Ned Flanders first appeared—and is the longest-running sitcom and animated television program in the United States, with more than six hundred episodes.

2. For a fuller treatment of Ned Flanders as both a satire and portrait of the American evangelical, see Pinsky, *Gospel according to* The Simpsons, 42–59, and Feltmate, "It's Funny," 232–38.

3. Feltmate, "It's Funny," 223. In addition to evangelicals, *The Simpsons* also satirizes Catholics, Jews, and Hindus.

4. "I Love Lisa," season 4, episode 15, *The Simpsons: The Complete Fourth Season,* DVD, written by Frank Mula (1993; Beverly Hills, CA: 20th Century Fox Home Entertainment, 2012).

5. See Matt Groening, *The Simpsons Uncensored Family Album* (New York: Harper Perennial, 1991), n.p.

6. This statue is also sometimes known as *The Praying Hands.* There is another 32-foot tall statue of oversized hands clasped in prayer in Webb City, Missouri, erected in 1972. (See "Giant Hands in Prayer," *Roadside America,* http://www.roadsideamerica.com/story/2916.)

7. Shepard, *Forgiven,* 310–11. For a description and image of the proposed Old Jerusalem park, see Bakker and Bakker, *Jim and Tammy Bakker,* 199, 203.

8. As quoted in William E. Schmidt, "TV Minister Calls His Resort 'Bait' for Christianity,"

*New York Times,* December 24, 1985, A8. Bakker articulated the same sentiment another way: "Jesus said, basically, that we were to be fishers of men. And with some of the bait that we have used in the church—I call it 'dill pickle religion'—I've never seen anyone catch a fish with a dill pickle and a sourpuss religion. We're using better bait to win people to Jesus Christ." As quoted in "Better Bait," *Christian Century* 102 (February 20, 1985): 178.

9. Moore, *Selling God,* 251.

10. See Bielo, *Ark Encounter,* 20–27, 85–109.

11. For an extensive history of the prosperity gospel in the United States, see Bowler, *Blessed.*

12. See Grubiak, "Architecture for the Electronic Church," 409–10.

13. Moore, *Selling God,* 251.

14. See "Western Artists: Hiram Powers," *Western Monthly Magazine* 3, no. 4 (April 1835): 246. I am grateful to Jerome Tharaud, author of the forthcoming *Apocalyptic Geographies: Religion, Media, and the American Landscape* (Princeton, NJ: Princeton University Press, 2020), for bringing this exhibit to my attention.

15. For an overview of biblical re-creations, see Bielo, *Ark Encounter,* 46–49, 50–52. For discussion of Jerusalem itself as a theme park, see Annabel Jane Wharton, *Selling Jerusalem: Relics, Replicas, Theme Parks* (Chicago: University of Chicago Press, 2006), 189–232.

16. See Long, *Imagining the Holy Land,* 7–41; Davis, *Landscape of Belief,* 89–97.

17. See Long, *Imagining the Holy Land,* 43–70; Davis, *Landscape of Belief,* 95–97.

18. Holy Land USA in Connecticut was featured by comedian and satirist Stephen Colbert. See "Colbert: Shrine of the Times," *The Daily Show,* Comedy Central (November 20, 2002). See also Bielo, *Ark Encounter,* 47. For an account of Holy Land USA in Bedford County, Virginia, see Beal, *Roadside Religion,* 25–48.

19. See Matthew Avery Sutton, *Aimee Semple McPherson and the Resurrection of Christian America* (Cambridge, MA: Harvard University Press, 2009).

20. For analysis of Schuller's conflation of religion with drive-in culture in the Garden Grove Community Church, see Erica Robles-Anderson, "The Crystal Cathedral: Architecture for Mediated Congregation," *Public Culture* 24, no. 3 (Fall 2012): 577–99; and Sylvia Lavin, "Richard Neutra and the Psychology of the American Spectator," *Grey Room* 1 (Fall 2000): 42–63.

21. See Beal, *Roadside Religion.* See also the website Roadside America (http://www.roadside america.com) for other sites of religious interest.

22. See Wigger, *PTL,* 89–90, 128.

23. For a description of the proposed Ministry Center as well as a rendering of it, see Bakker and Bakker, *Jim and Tammy Bakker,* 198–99; and Schmidt, "TV Minister," A8. In addition to London's Crystal Palace, Bakker's Ministry Center may have also been inspired by architect Philip Johnson's Crystal Cathedral (1977–81) in Garden Grove, California, for the Reverend

Robert Schuller, but the historicist architecture of Bakker's proposal was directly aligned with Paxton's 1851 design. In addition to the crystalline Ministry Center, Bakker also imagined a multistory, decagonal Crystal Tower to house people coming to the Ministry Center. For an image of this tower, see Bakker and Bakker, *Jim and Tammy Bakker,* 200.

24. Edward B. Fiske, "The Oral Roberts Empire," *New York Times Magazine,* April 22, 1973, 17.

25. As quoted in O'Guinn and Belk, "Heaven on Earth," 232–33.

26. Shepard makes these comparisons (see Shepard, *Forgiven,* 235). See also Wigger, *PTL,* 168–69, for more detail on these connections to Disney. Heritage USA's King's Castle (now demolished) housed what was reportedly the world's largest Wendy's fast food restaurant and also at one point had a go-kart track. Its architectural flatness made it look amateurish compared to the Sleeping Beauty Castle at Disneyland and Cinderella Castle at Disney World. See Wigger, *PTL,* 222–23.

27. Shepard, *Forgiven,* 250.

28. Shepard, *Forgiven,* 235.

29. See, for example, Angela Elwell Hunt, "It's All You Heard and More . . . Heritage USA," *Fundamentalist Journal* 6, no. 5 (May 1987): 21; and Megan Rosenfeld, "Heritage USA and the Heavenly Vacation: South Carolina Park Caters to Born-Again Christians," *Washington Post,* June 15, 1986, H1.

30. As quoted in FitzGerald, "Reflections," 87.

31. See, for example, Mazur and Koda, "The Happiest Place on Earth," 299–315. For a counterpoint, see Margaret R. Miles, "Disney Spirituality: An Oxymoron?" *Christian Spirituality Bulletin* (Spring 1999): 13–18.

32. For an extended analysis of Heritage USA vis-à-vis Eliade's and others' concepts of the sacred, see O'Guinn and Belk, "Heaven on Earth," 229–35.

33. As quoted in FitzGerald, "Reflections," 80.

34. Beth Macklin, "ORU Campus Has Hollywood Atmosphere in TV Filming," *Tulsa World,* July 16, 1969, clipping in "Oral Roberts University—Radio and Television" vertical file, Tulsa City-County Library, Tulsa, OK.

35. Bakker and Bakker, *Jim and Tammy Bakker,* 13, as also quoted in FitzGerald, "Reflections," 80.

36. For examples of firsthand accounts of visitors to Heritage USA, see Peter S. Hawkins, "American Heritage," in *One Nation under God? Religion and American Culture,* ed. Marjorie Garber and Rebecca L. Walkowitz (New York: Routledge, 1999), 258–79; FitzGerald, "Reflections," 45–87; Hunt, "It's All You Heard," 21; and Rosenfeld, "Heritage USA," H1, H8–H9. See also Wigger, *PTL,* 222–24.

37. Rosenfeld, "Heritage USA," H8.

38. For an extensive accounting of Jim Bakker's rise and fall, with particular emphasis on the financial scandal, see Shepard, *Forgiven.* For another analysis of the PTL and more on the creation of Heritage USA, see Wigger, *PTL.*

39. As Frances FitzGerald observed, "Just as a matter of geography, I found it hard to figure out a religious center to Heritage USA" (FitzGerald, "Reflections," 80).

40. For an image of the Barn Auditorium, see Bakker and Bakker, *Jim and Tammy Bakker,* 96.

41. A large, elaborate Victorian-style home called "Kevin's House" became an object of scandal after it was revealed it did not house disabled children, just Kevin and his relatives. See Shepard, *Forgiven,* 415–16.

42. For a description of the buildings at Heritage USA related to the Heritage Village Church ministry and Christian community, see Bakker and Bakker, *Jim and Tammy Bakker,* 88–123.

43. Bakker and Bakker, *Jim and Tammy Bakker,* 89, 91.

44. Bakker and Bakker, *Jim and Tammy Bakker,* 92.

45. For images of this rustic architecture, see Bakker and Bakker, *Jim and Tammy Bakker,* 93–95, 121.

46. For an understanding of the use of Colonial Revival architecture throughout American architectural history, see Richard Guy Wilson and Shaun Eyring, eds., *Re-Creating the American Past: Essays on the Colonial Revival* (Charlottesville: University of Virginia Press, 2006).

47. Shepard, *Forgiven,* 66.

48. Hawkins, "American Heritage," 261.

49. For the long history of the architectural co-opting of George Washington's Mount Vernon, see Lydia Mattice Brandt, *First in the Homes of His Countrymen: George Washington's Mount Vernon in the American Imagination* (Charlottesville: University of Virginia Press, 2016).

50. Bakker and Bakker, *Jim and Tammy Bakker,* 168, including an image of the Billy Graham childhood home at Heritage USA, which was moved again to its current location at the Billy Graham Library in Charlotte, NC.

51. Bakker and Bakker, *Jim and Tammy Bakker,* 98.

52. See Umberto Eco, *Travels in Hyper Reality: Essays,* trans. William Weaver (San Diego: Harcourt Brace Jovanovich, 1986).

53. Bakker and Bakker, *Jim and Tammy Bakke,* 202. See page 203 for an image of the proposed Old Jerusalem park.

54. FitzGerald, "Reflections," 87.

55. Bakker and Bakker, *Jim and Tammy Bakker,* 129.

56. O'Guinn and Belk, "Heaven on Earth," 236.

57. O'Guinn and Belk, "Heaven on Earth, 237.

58. As quoted in Bakker and Bakker, *Jim and Tammy Bakker,* 196.

59. For an analysis of Jerry Falwell, particularly his fundamentalism and engagement in American political life, see Harding, *Book of Jerry Falwell.* Before a sexual scandal over his visits to prostitutes emerged in 1988, Pentecostal preacher Jimmy Swaggart wanted to take over PTL, but Bakker had put his trust in Falwell. In a 1987 interview with Ted Koppel, Bakker claimed that he had "made a terrible mistake" and that he believed Falwell wanted to "steal Heritage USA and my ministry" (as quoted in Wigger, *PTL,* 290).

60. For video of the event as well as Falwell's comments after his fall, see jamesKI4JKV, "PTL Jerry Falwell Goes Down Waterslide," filmed September 10, 1987, YouTube video, 9:24 minutes, posted February 7, 2012, https://youtu.be/OHVBYR9RPyM.

61. See, for example, United Press International, "Falwell Was All Dressed Up with Someplace Wet to Go," *Chicago Tribune,* September 12, 1987; and "Fund Raising: Falwell Hits the Skids," *Time,* September 21, 1987.

62. Sharon Perkinson, "The Rev. Jerry Falwell, Who Once Vowed There Would . . . ," United Press International Archives, September 10, 1987, https://upi.com/4806213.

63. Quoted in Perkinson, "Rev. Jerry Falwell.

64. As quoted in Associated Press, "Falwell Keeps Vow, Tackles Water Slide," *Register-Guard* (Eugene, OR), September 11, 1987, 11A.

65. As quoted in Perkinson, "Rev. Jerry Falwell."

66. Associated Press, "Falwell Keeps Vow."

67. See jamesKI4JKV, "PTL Jerry Falwell."

68. As quoted in Roberto Suro, "The Papal Visit: Pontiff Embraces Welcome in Miami, Deflects Queries," *New York Times,* September 11, 1987, A01.

69. The *New York Times* noted this difference in approaches between the pope and the Reverend Falwell in John Corry, "TV: No One Steals the Pope's Scenes," *New York Times,* September 12, 1987, 54.

70. See jamesKI4JKV, "PTL Jerry Falwell."

71. As quoted in Associated Press, "Falwell Keeps Vow."

72. Corry, "TV," 54.

73. Harding, *Book of Jerry Falwell,* 259.

74. Harding, *Book of Jerry Falwell,* 259.

75. Sandra G. Boodman, "How Falwell Raises His Millions: The Fund-Raising Technique," *Washington Post,* June 28, 1981.

76. Harding, *Book of Jerry Falwell,* 258.

77. As quoted in United Press International, "Falwell Was All Dressed Up."

78. For a journalistic firsthand account of the end of the PTL, see Hunter James, *Smile Pretty and Say Jesus: The Last Great Days of the PTL* (Athens: University of Georgia Press, 1993). See also Wigger, *PTL,* 295–97.

79. Commentary on "I'm Goin' to Praiseland," season 12, episode 19, *The Simpsons: The Complete Twelfth Season,* DVD, written by Julie Thacker (2001; Beverly Hills, California: 20th Century Fox Home Entertainment, 2009). The episode aired three months after the opening of Holy Land Experience in Orlando, Florida, which may have also informed the idea of Praiseland. See Pinsky, *Gospel according to* The Simpsons, 56.

80. "I'm Goin' to Praiseland."

81. Pinksy, *Gospel according to* The Simpsons, 56.

82. "I'm Goin' to Praiseland."

83. See Harrell, *All Things Are Possible,* 11–12.

84. For a more detailed study of Oral Roberts University's architecture and its connection to the electronic church, see Grubiak, "Architecture for the Electronic Church."

85. As quoted in Harrell, *Oral Roberts,* 227 (original source unclear); and Fiske, "Oral Roberts Empire," 17.

86. "Oral Roberts to Open Crusade," *Seattle Times,* May 7, 1963, 12.

87. For an analysis and history of the U.S. Science Pavilion, see Gyure, *Minoru Yamasaki,* 160–63.

88. While not a trained architect or builder, Oral Roberts had an active role in the design of his campus. As architect Frank Wallace recounted, Roberts talked twice a week with him when Roberts was in town. See Bob Foresman, "ORU Architect Gaining Repute," *Tulsa Tribune,* March 2, 1979, 2F, clipping in "Oral Roberts University—Buildings" vertical file, Tulsa City-County Library, Tulsa, OK.

89. Peter C. Papademetriou, "O.R.U. Architecture?," *Progressive Architecture* 59 (June 1978): 52.

90. Andrew Preston, *Sword of the Spirit, Shield of Faith: Religion in American War and Diplomacy* (New York: Alfred A. Knopf, 2012), 468.

91. As quoted in John M. Findlay, *Magic Lands: Western Cityscapes and American Culture after 1940* (Berkeley: University of California Press, 1992), 237.

92. For a more detailed discussion on the Seattle fair and its engagement with the Cold War and religion, see Findlay, *Magic Lands.* For more discussion on religion's perceived role in the Cold War, see James Gilbert, *Redeeming Culture: American Religion in an Age of Science* (Chicago: University of Chicago Press, 1997); Jonathan P. Herzog, *The Spiritual-Industrial Complex: America's Religious Battle against Communism in the Early Cold War* (New York:

Oxford University Press, 2011); and David F. Noble, *The Religion of Technology: The Divinity of Man and the Spirit of Invention* (New York: Alfred A. Knopf, 1998).

93. Papademetriou, "O.R.U. Architecture?," 53, 55; and Larry van Dyne, "God and Man at Oral Roberts," *Chronicle of Higher Education,* December 8, 1975, 3. On New Formalism, see Gyure, *Minoru Yamasaki,* 126–27.

94. Papademetriou, "O.R.U. Architecture?," 55.

95. Thomas Hine, *Populuxe* (New York: Alfred A. Knopf, 1984), 12.

96. Granville Oral Roberts, *Oral Roberts University, 1965–1983, "True to a Heavenly Vision"* (New York: Newcomen Society of the United States, 1983), 15.

97. There were several designs for the Prayer Tower. In 1962, when Cecil Stanfield was the architect for the campus, Oral Roberts University published a campus master plan with a central structure in a triangular, sail-like shape (see Bob Foresman, "Roberts Details 4-Year University Plans," *Tulsa Tribune,* November 26, 1962, 17, clipping in "Oral Roberts University—Buildings" vertical file, Tulsa City-County Library, Tulsa, OK). The design changed dramatically after Oral Roberts visited Seattle in 1963 and changed his architect to Frank Wallace. In a second scheme published in 1964, Wallace transformed the central structure, now named the Prayer Tower, into an open cylinder with lancet arches and an open crown (see "New University Shaping Up Fast," *Tulsa Daily World,* July 8, 1964, 1, clipping in "Oral Roberts University—Buildings" vertical file, Tulsa City-County Library, Tulsa, OK). In total, there were a reported five schemes for the Prayer Tower (see "The Way We Weren't," *Perihelion* (Tulsa, OK: Oral Roberts University), 1976, 86). This design borrowed much formal language from Yamasaki's "space Gothic" arches on the Seattle fairgrounds.

98. The Seattle Space Needle was modeled after the Fernsehturm (1954–56) radio and television tower in Stuttgart, Germany, notable for its rotating restaurant (see Karrie Jacobs, "Would We Take the Space Needle Seriously If It Had Been Designed by Buckminster Fuller?," *Metropolis* 10 (May 1991): 118; and Knute Berger, *Space Needle: The Spirit of Seattle* (Seattle: Documentary Media, 2012)). One of the Seattle fair organizers who had visited the Stuttgart tower suggested that the fair have a similar structure with a similar rotating feature. The Seattle Space Needle did not have radio or television broadcasting capabilities, but during the world's fair it did host a carillon, which the Prayer Tower emulated.

99. Fiske, "Oral Roberts Empire," 17.

100. Roberts, *Oral Roberts University,* 15.

101. Other American college and university campuses have tall, centralizing structures such as campaniles and towers, for example, the University of Texas's library tower, Yale University's Harkness Tower, and the University of Pittsburgh's Cathedral of Learning. For religiously affiliated colleges and universities, their church spires operate as visual cues of religion's centrality.

Yet a tower dedicated to prayer in the sense of Oral Roberts University's Prayer Tower is rare. To understand Oral Roberts University's Prayer Tower in the context of American campus design, see Paul V. Turner, *Campus: An American Planning Tradition* (Cambridge, MA: MIT Press and the Architectural History Foundation, 1987); and Grubiak, *White Elephants on Campus.*

102. Harrell, *Oral Roberts,* 333.

103. As quoted in United Press International, "Four Years of Donations Built $120 Million Hospital of Faith," *New York Times,* October 20, 1981, A24.

104. For an account of the battle over the City of Faith, see Harrell, *Oral Roberts,* 383–88.

105. As quoted in United Press International, "Four Years of Donations," A24.

106. Roberts, "I Must Tell Somebody," 10.

107. "A Cross to Bear," *Saturday Oklahoman and Times* (Oklahoma City), December 19, 1981, 19.

108. Associated Press, "Oral Roberts Vigil Ends in New Plea for Funds," *New York Times,* April 1, 1987, A21.

109. As quoted in Randy Frame, "Fund Raising: Did Oral Roberts Go Too Far?," *Christianity Today,* February 20, 1987.

110. Garry Trudeau, *Doonesbury,* cartoon, February 4, 1987, http://www.gocomics.com /doonesbury/1987/02/04.

111. Garry Trudeau, *Doonesbury,* cartoon, February 5, 1987, http://www.gocomics.com /doonesbury/1987/02/05.

112. Associated Press, "Oral Roberts Vigil Ends."

113. These musicals include *The Gospel According to Tammy Faye* (2006), *Big Tent* (2007), and the proposed *Rise* (2012).

114. *Religulous,* directed by Larry Charles (2008; Santa Monica, CA: Lionsgate, 2009), DVD.

115. See, for example, Tim Funk, "Fallen PTL Preacher Jim Bakker Is Back with a New Message about the Apocalypse," *Charlotte Observer,* February 17, 2018, https://www.charlotte observer.com/living/religion/article200297074.html; and Chris Morris, "Disgraced Televangelist Jim Bakker Is Now Selling Real Estate and $150 Water Bottles," *Fortune Magazine,* May 7, 2018, http://fortune.com/2018/05/07/televangelist-jim-bakker-prepper-selling-real-estate -water-bottle-apocalypse/. A *Daily Mail* article compared Bakker's Morningside Church to a theme park. See "EXCLUSIVE: Inside Jim Bakker's Missouri Town Prepping for the Nuclear Apocalypse and ECLIPSE Fallout—Where People Come to Stock Up on Freeze-Dried Meals and Idolize the TV Preacher Who Was Jailed for Fraud and Accused of Rape," *Daily Mail* (London), August 21, 2017, https://www.dailymail.co.uk/news/article-4790432/Inside-Jim

-Bakker-Missouri-town-prepping-Apocalypse.html. On Morningside Church, see also Ketchell, *Holy Hills of the Ozarks,* xii–xiii.

## 4. CHARLES DARWIN'S NIGHT AT THE CREATION MUSEUM

1. "The Dumbest People, Events and Things of 2007," *MAD* magazine, January 2008.

2. For an overview of creationist belief and the history of its development, see Numbers, *Creationists.*

3. As quoted in Czarina Ong, "Ozzy Osbourne Visits the Ark Encounter, Staff Say They 'Paid Some Very Nice Compliments,'" *Christian Today,* December 16, 2017, https://www .christiantoday.com/article/ozzy-osbourne-visits-the-ark-encounter-staff-say-they-paid-some -very-nice-compliments/121483.htm.

4. See Jonathan P. Hill, "National Study of Religion and Human Origins," BioLogos, December 2, 2014, https://biologos.org/articles/the-recipe-for-creationism. I am grateful to James Bielo for bringing this study to my attention.

5. Trollinger and Trollinger, *Righting America,* 1–2. Also on the Creation Museum, see Stevenson, *Sensational Devotion,* 128–61.

6. For an understanding of Ken Ham, see Randall J. Stephens and Karl W. Giberson, *The Anointed: Evangelical Truth in a Secular Age* (Cambridge, MA: Belknap Press of Harvard University Press, 2011).

7. As quoted in Trollinger and Trollinger, *Righting America,* 12–13.

8. Laurie Goodstein, "A Noah's Ark in Kentucky, Dinosaurs Included," *New York Times,* June 26, 2016, A13; Trollinger and Trollinger, *Righting America,* 13.

9. For a summary discussion on Answers in Genesis as it relates to Christian fundamental-ism, see Trollinger and Trollinger, *Righting America,* 2–13; see 313–16 for a useful list of readings related to Christian fundamentalism. For a history of Christian fundamentalism in America, see Marsden, *Fundamentalism and American Culture;* and Ernest R. Sandeen, *The Roots of Fundamentalism: British and American Millenarianism, 1800–1930* (Chicago: University of Chicago Press, 1970).

10. Trollinger and Trollinger, *Righting America,* 42–51.

11. Trollinger and Trollinger, *Righting America,* 31–32, 52–54, 157–64. See also Casey Ryan Kelly and Kristen E. Hoerl, "Genesis in Hyperreality: Legitimizing Disingenuous Controversy at the Creation Museum," *Argumentation and Advocacy* 48, no. 3 (2012): 131–32.

12. Trollinger and Trollinger, *Righting America,* 50–51.

13. Trollinger and Trollinger, *Righting America,* 192–96.

14. Goodstein, "Noah's Ark in Kentucky."

15. Trollinger and Trollinger, *Righting America,* 57–58.

16. Trollinger and Trollinger, *Righting America,* 196–98. See also Answers in Genesis, "Dragons: Fact or Fable?," n.d., https://answersingenesis.org/dinosaurs/dragon-legends/dragons-fact-or-fable/.

17. Trollinger and Trollinger, *Righting America,* 68.

18. Trollinger and Trollinger, *Righting America,* 67–73.

19. Kelly and Hoerl, "Genesis in Hyperreality," 130.

20. Kelly and Hoerl, "Genesis in Hyperreality," 126. Emphasis in the original.

21. For a deeper discussion of how the Creation Museum appropriates the authority of natural history museums in name and in display techniques, see Trollinger and Trollinger, *Righting America,* 16–63; and Kelly and Hoerl, "Genesis in Hyperreality," 123–41. For more on the Creation Museum's use of the visual rhetoric of secular scientific methods, see Larissa Carneiro, "Emulating Science: The Rhetorical Figures of Creationism," *Journal for Religion, Film and Media* 3, no. 2 (2017): 53–64.

22. Trollinger and Trollinger, *Righting America,* 11–12.

23. Creation Museum, "Creation Museum Lands Major Architectural Firm—A. M. Kinney!," June 2, 2000, https://creationmuseum.org/blog/2000/06/02/creation-museum-lands-major-architectural-firm-am-kinney/.

24. A. A. Gill, "Roll Over, Charles Darwin!" *Vanity Fair,* February 2010, https://www.vanityfair.com/news/2010/02/creation-museum-201002.

25. For an understanding of the architecture of the American megachurch and its appeal to commercial and vernacular forms, see Jeanne Halgren Kilde, "Reading Megachurches: Investigating the Religious and Cultural Work of Church," in *American Sanctuary: Understanding Sacred Spaces,* ed. Louis P. Nelson (Bloomington: Indiana University Press, 2006), 225–49; and Charity R. Carney, "Sanctifying the SUV: Megachurches, the Prosperity Gospel, and the Suburban Christian," in *Making Suburbia: New Histories of Everyday America,* ed. John Archer, John J. P. Sandul, and Katherine Solomonson (Minneapolis: University of Minnesota Press, 2015), 240–57.

26. Gill, "Roll Over, Charles Darwin!"

27. For a discussion of the idea of religious kitsch, see F. B. Brown, *Good Taste, Bad Taste,* 128–59, with an analysis of the idea applied to the Precious Moments Chapel in Carthage, Missouri. See also McDannell, *Material Christianity,* 163; and Promey, *Sensational Religion,* 6.

28. Bielo, *Ark Encounter,* 29.

29. For a firsthand account of the debate, see Bielo, *Ark Encounter,* 110–13. See also Trollinger and Trollinger, *Righting America,* 64–67. For video of the debate, see Answers in Genesis,

"Bill Nye Debates Ken Ham," YouTube video, 2:45:32 hours, streamed live February 4, 2014, https://youtu.be/z6kgvhG3AkI.

30. Bill Nye, *Undeniable: Evolution and the Science of Creation,* ed. Corey S. Powell (New York: St. Martin's Griffin, 2014), 9–18.

31. For a fuller treatment of the Scopes Trial, Christian fundamentalism, and the emergence of a crisis of faith wrought by Charles Darwin's thesis, see Paul K. Conkin, *When All the Gods Trembled: Darwinism, Scopes, and American Intellectuals* (Lanham, MD: Rowman & Littlefield, 1998).

32. Trollinger and Trollinger, *Righting America,* 65.

33. Michael Schulson, "The Bill Nye–Ken Ham Debate Was a Nightmare for Science," *Daily Beast,* February 5, 2014, https://www.thedailybeast.com/the-bill-nye-ken-ham-debate-was-a-nightmare-for-science, emphasis in the original, as quoted in Trollinger and Trollinger, *Righting America,* 65.

34. For example, in *The Simpsons* 2006 episode "The Monkey Suit" based on the Scopes Trial, Lisa Simpson, the show's archetype of an intelligent, liberal person, protests the closing of an exhibit on evolution prompted by her evangelical neighbor, Ned Flanders.

35. As quoted in Gordy Slack, "Inside the Creation Museum," *Salon,* May 31, 2007, https://www.salon.com/2007/05/31/creation_museum/.

36. Yanni, *Nature's Museums,* 88.

37. As quoted in Yanni, *Nature's Museums,* 88.

38. Yanni, *Nature's Museums,* 88.

39. As quoted in Yanni, *Nature's Museums,* 88.

40. For a detailed architectural history of the Oxford Museum of Natural History, see Eve Blau, *Ruskinian Gothic: The Architecture of Deane and Woodward, 1845–1861* (Princeton, NJ: Princeton University Press, 1982), 48–81.

41. Yanni, *Nature's Museums,* 63.

42. Yanni, *Nature's Museums,* 86.

43. See Yanni, *Nature's Museums,* 85–86.

44. "Dumbest People, Events and Things."

45. Michael D. Slaubaugh, "Mad Magazine Circulation Figures 1961 to 2017," http://users.pfw.edu/slaubau/madcirc.htm.

46. For a history of the magazine, see Maria Reidelbach, *Completely* MAD: *A History of the Comic Book and Magazine* (Boston: Little, Brown, 1991); for an interpretation of its Jewish origins, see Nathan Abrams, "A Secular Talmud: The Jewish Sensibility of *MAD* Magazine," *Studies in American Humor* 30 (2014): 111–22.

47. The cartoon was mentioned in Theresa Sanders, *Approaching Eden: Adam and Eve in Popular Culture* (Lanham, MD: Rowman & Littlefield, 2009), 129.

48. In another example of a visual critique of creationist beliefs, James Bielo examines a cartoon published in 2005 in the *Columbia (MO) Daily Tribune* that satirizes the "Kansas School Board of Edukashen" (a reference to the 2005 debates on evolution and creationism in public education in Kansas) embodied in a male figure Bielo describes as "racialized poor whiteness" with "bare feet, tattered overalls, misshapen physical features, pot belly, and grossly nonstandard spelling." To this figure of a creationist believer, a figure of God, patterned after Michelangelo's *The Creation of Adam* painting in the Sistine Chapel, says "Good God, Boy! You're the best argument *against* 'intelligent' design I've ever seen!" See Bielo, *Ark Encounter,* 170–71, including a reproduction of the cartoon.

49. Bielo, *Ark Encounter,* 21, 178.

50. Bielo, *Ark Encounter,* 179.

51. Quoted in Karen Heller, "A Giant Ark Is Just the Start. These Creationists Have a Bigger Plan for Recruiting New Believers," *Washington Post,* May 24, 2017.

52. Goodstein, "Noah's Ark in Kentucky."

53. Quoted in Heller, "Giant Ark Is Just the Start."

54. Heller, "Giant Ark Is Just the Start."

55. Heller, "Giant Ark Is Just the Start."

56. Quoted in Jessica Contrera, "Bill Nye Visited a Noah's Ark He Doesn't Believe Should Exist," *Washington Post,* July 10, 2016.

57. Venturi, Brown, and Izenour, *Learning from Las Vegas.*

58. Quoted in Mark Wilson, "I Built Noah's $100 Million Ark," *Fast Company Design,* July 11, 2016, https://www.fastcodesign.com/3061679/i-built-noahs-100-million-ark.

59. Amanda Petruish, "A Boat of Biblical Proportions," *Atlantic,* December 2012, https://www.theatlantic.com/magazine/archive/2012/12/a-boat-of-biblical-proportions/309173/, as quoted in Trollinger and Trollinger, *Righting America,* 232–33.

60. See Ark Encounter, "What's New at the Ark Encounter?," November 29, 2016, https://arkencounter.com/blog/2016/11/29/whats-new-at-the-ark-encounter/.

61. The Trollingers make this argument about the door of the ark as the material realization of God's judgment in the view of Answers in Genesis in Trollinger and Trollinger, *Righting America,* 228–35.

62. Goodstein, "Noah's Ark in Kentucky."

63. Trollinger and Trollinger, *Righting America,* 67; Ken Ham, @aigkenham, Twitter post, June 7, 2016, 2:50 a.m., https://twitter.com/aigkenham/status/740118795713425408.

64. See the list maintained by James Bielo at "Materializing the Bible," https://www.materializingthebible.com/creationist-sites.html.

65. Jeffrey Lee Puckett, "Ozzy Visits the Ark Encounter and Doesn't Suffer the Wrath of God," *Louisville (KY) Courier-Journal,* December 20, 2017, https://www.courier-journal.com/story/news/local/2017/12/20/ozzy-osbourne-visits-ark-encounter-kentucky/968417001/.

66. Quoted in Andy Webster, "Review: 'Bill Nye: Science Guy,' a Portrait of a Fighter for Facts," *New York Times,* October 27, 2017, C8, https://www.nytimes.com/2017/10/26/movies/bill-nye-science-guy-review-documentary.html.


## 5. GUMBY JESUS

1. On the *Christus* statue, see John G. Turner, *The Mormon Jesus: A Biography* (Cambridge, MA: Harvard University Press, 2016), 269–73. The Mormon *Christus* statues are replicas of Bertel Thorvaldsen's *Christus* statue (1821–1838) in Copenhagen, Denmark, which Jim Bakker also replicated for *The Resurrected Christ* statue.

2. On the Ozark religious tourism landscape, see Ketchell, *Holy Hills of the Ozarks.*

3. Smith, *Story of the Statue,* 5; also quoted in John Fergus Ryan, "Twilight Years of a Kindly Old Hatesmith," *Esquire,* August 1968, 88.

4. As quoted in Ryan, "Twilight Years," 91.

5. As quoted in Trillin, "U.S. Journal," 70.

6. For a biography of Gerald L. K. Smith, see Jeansonne, *Gerald L. K. Smith.*

7. As quoted in Trillin, "U.S. Journal," 69.

8. "A Monument to Himself," *Time,* July 22, 1966, 23; Trillin, "U.S. Journal," 69.

9. "A Monument to Himself," 23.

10. "A Monument to Himself," 23. In his biography of Smith, Jeansonne echoed this interpretation: "Masquerading as a monument to Christ, Smith intended it in reality as a monument to himself" (Jeansonne, *Gerald L. K. Smith,* 205).

11. Burke Long makes this same observation about visitors to the statue not understanding its creator's beliefs. For Long's interpretation of the "Sacred Projects," see Long, *Imagining the Holy Land,* 70–87.

12. See Jeansonne, *Gerald L. K. Smith,* 193–98. On the Passion play, see also Stevenson, *Sensational Devotion,* 98–127.

13. As quoted in Trillin, "U.S. Journal," 78. For Smith's plans for the New Holy Land, see Jeansonne, *Gerald L. K. Smith,* 202–3.

14. For a detailed description and interpretation of the Holy Land Tour, see Long, *Imagining the Holy Land,* 76–87.

15. As quoted in Jeansonne, *Gerald L. K. Smith,* 202.

16. As quoted in Trillin, "U.S. Journal," 70.

17. As quoted in Ernest Dumas, "Gerald L. K. Smith Becomes Issue in Ozarks," *New York Times,* November 28, 1969, 30.

18. As quoted in Associated Press, "Jewish Group Asks Nixon to Bar Fund for Road in Ozarks," *New York Times,* January 25, 1970, 48.

19. Trillin, "U.S. Journal," 76.

20. Jeansonne, *Gerald L. K. Smith,* 201.

21. Sullivan was also said to have worked as an assistant to sculptor Gutzon Borglum on Mount Rushmore in South Dakota, though it is unclear if this was true. See, for example, Ryan, "Twilight Years," 88.

22. Edgar A. Albin, "The Colossal Ungainly Christ on Arkansas's Magnetic Mountain," *St. Louis Post-Dispatch,* June 20, 1971; also cited in Jeansonne, *Gerald L. K. Smith,* 192.

23. See Ketchell, *Holy Hills of the Ozarks.* On Samuel Butcher's Precious Moments Chapel, see Ketchell, "Precious Moments Chapel"; and Beal, *Roadside Religion,* 135–58. On the Precious Moments Chapel as religious kitsch, see F. B. Brown, *Good Taste, Bad Taste,* 128–59. On religious kitsch generally, see McDannell, *Material Christianity,* 163; and Promey, *Sensational Religion,* 6.

24. Albin, "Colossal Ungainly Christ."

# SELECTED BIBLIOGRAPHY

Albanese, Catherine L. "Religion and Popular Culture: An Introductory Essay." *Journal of the American Academy of Religion* 59, no. 4 (Fall 1996): 733–42.

Baker, William J. *Playing with God: Religion and Modern Sport.* Cambridge, MA: Harvard University Press, 2007.

Bakker, Jim, and Tammy Faye Bakker. *Jim and Tammy Bakker Present the Ministries of Heritage Village Church.* Charlotte, NC: Heritage Village Church and Missionary Fellowship, 1986.

Beal, Timothy. *Roadside Religion: In Search of the Sacred, the Strange, and the Substance of Faith.* Boston: Beacon Press, 2005.

Berger, Peter L. *Redeeming Laughter: The Comic Dimension of Human Experience.* 2nd ed. Berlin: Walter de Gruyter, 2014. First published 1997.

Bielo, James S. *Ark Encounter: The Making of a Creationist Theme Park.* New York: New York University Press, 2018.

Bowler, Kate. *Blessed: A History of the American Prosperity Gospel.* New York: Oxford University Press, 2013.

Brown, Frank Burch. *Good Taste, Bad Taste, and Christian Taste.* New York: Oxford University Press, 2000.

Carter, Thomas. *Building Zion: The Material World of Mormon Settlement.* Minneapolis: University of Minnesota Press, 2014.

Chidester, David. *Authentic Fakes: Religion and American Popular Culture.* Berkeley: University of California Press, 2005.

Clotfelter, Charles T. *Big-Time Sports in American Universities.* New York: Cambridge University Press, 2011.

Davis, John. *The Landscape of Belief: Encountering the Holy Land in Nineteenth-Century American Art and Culture.* Princeton, NJ: Princeton University Press, 1996.

Eire, Carlos M. N. *War against the Idols: The Reformation of Worship from Erasmus to Calvin.* Cambridge: Cambridge University Press, 1986.

Eliade, Mircea. *The Sacred and the Profane: The Nature of Religion.* Trans. William R. Trask. San Diego: Harcourt, 1959, 1987.

Feltmate, David. *Drawn to the Gods: Religion and Humor in* The Simpsons, South Park*, and* Family Guy. New York: New York University Press, 2017.

———. "It's Funny Because It's True? The Simpsons, Satire, and the Significance of Religious Humor in Popular Culture." *Journal of the American Academy of Religion* 81, no. 1 (March 2013): 222–48.

———. "Religion and Humor: A Bibliography." *Bulletin for the Study of Religion* 42, no. 3 (August 2013): 47–48.

FitzGerald, Frances. "Reflections: Jim and Tammy." *New Yorker* (April 23, 1990): 45–87.

Forbes, Bruce David, and Jeffery H. Mahan, eds. *Religion and Popular Culture in America.* Rev. ed. Berkeley: University of California Press, 2005.

Geertz, Clifford. "Religion as a Cultural System." In *Anthropological Approaches to the Study of Religion,* ed. Michael Banton, 1–46. London: Tavistock, 1966. Reprinted in Geertz, *The Interpretation of Cultures,* 87–125. New York: Basic Books, 1973.

Givens, Terryl L. *People of Paradox: A History of Mormon Culture.* New York: Oxford University Press, 2007.

Grubiak, Margaret M. "An Architecture for the Electronic Church: Oral Roberts University in Tulsa, Oklahoma." *Technology and Culture* 57, no. 2 (April 2016): 380–413.

———. "Visualizing the Modern Catholic University: The Original Intention of 'Touchdown Jesus' at the University of Notre Dame." *Material Religion* 6, no. 3 (November 2010): 336–68.

———. *White Elephants on Campus: The Decline of the University Chapel in America, 1925–1965.* Notre Dame, IN: University of Notre Dame Press, 2014.

Harding, Susan Friend. *The Book of Jerry Falwell: Fundamentalist Language and Politics.* Princeton, NJ: Princeton University Press, 2000.

———. "Representing Fundamentalism: The Problem of the Repugnant Cultural Other." *Social Research* 58, no. 2 (Summer 1991): 373–93.

Harrell, David Edwin, Jr. *All Things Are Possible: The Healing and Charismatic Revivals in Modern America.* Bloomington: Indiana University Press, 1975.

———. *Oral Roberts: An American Life.* Bloomington: Indiana University Press, 1985.

Haws, J. B. *The Mormon Image in the American Mind: Fifty Years of Public Perception.* New York: Oxford University Press, 2013.

Higgs, Robert J. *God in the Stadium: Sports and Religion in America.* Lexington: University Press of Kentucky, 1995.

Hoffman, Shirl James. *Good Game: Christianity and the Culture of Sports.* Waco, Texas: Baylor University Press, 2010.

Hofstadter, Richard. *Anti-Intellectualism in American Life.* New York: Alfred A. Knopf, 1966.

Hyers, M. Conrad, ed. *Holy Laughter: Essays on Religion in the Comic Perspective.* New York: Seabury Press, 1969.

Jeansonne, Glen. *Gerald L. K. Smith: Minister of Hate.* New Haven, CT: Yale University Press, 1988.

Kantra, Robert A. *All Things Vain: Religious Satirists and Their Art.* University Park: Pennsylvania State University Press, 1984.

Ketchell, Aaron K. *Holy Hills of the Ozarks: Religion and Tourism in Branson, Missouri.* Baltimore: Johns Hopkins University Press, 2007.

———. "The Precious Moments Chapel: Suffering, Salvation, and the World's Most Popular Collectible." *Journal of American Culture* 22, no. 3 (Fall 1999): 27–33.

Leone, Mark P. "The New Mormon Temple in Washington, D.C." In *Historical Archaeology and the Importance of Material Things,* ed. Leland Ferguson, 46–47, 53. Rockville, MD: Society for Historical Archaeology, 1977.

Lindvall, Terry. *God Mocks: A History of Religious Satire from the Hebrew Prophets to Stephen Colbert.* New York: New York University Press, 2015.

Lippy, Charles. *Being Religious, American Style: A History of Popular Religiosity in the United States.* Westport, CT: Greenwood Press, 1994.

Long, Burke O. *Imagining the Holy Land: Maps, Models, and Fantasy Travels.* Bloomington: Indiana University Press, 2002.

Marsden, George M. *Fundamentalism and American Culture: The Shaping of Twentieth-Century Evangelicalism, 1870–1925.* New York: Oxford University Press, 1980.

Mazur, Eric Michael, and Kate McCarthy, eds. *God in the Details: American Religion in Popular Culture.* New York: Routledge, 2001.

McDannell, Colleen. *Material Christianity: Religion and Popular Culture in America.* New Haven, CT: Yale University Press, 1995.

Moore, R. Laurence. *Religious Outsiders and the Making of Americans.* Oxford: Oxford University Press, 1986.

———. *Selling God: American Religion and the Marketplace of Culture.* New York: Oxford University Press, 1994.

———. *Touchdown Jesus: The Mixing of Sacred and Secular in American History.* Louisville, KY: Westminster John Knox Press, 2003.

Morgan, David, ed. *Icons of American Protestantism: The Art of Warner Sallman.* New Haven, CT: Yale University Press, 1996.

———. *Religion and Material Culture: The Matter of Belief.* London: Routledge, 2010.

———. *The Sacred Gaze: Religious Visual Culture in Theory and Practice.* Berkeley: University of California Press, 2005.

———. *Visual Piety: A History and Theory of Popular Religious Images.* Berkeley: University of California Press, 1998.

Morgan, David, and Sally M. Promey, eds. *The Visual Culture of American Religions.* Berkeley: University of California Press, 2001.

Noll, Mark. *The Scandal of the Evangelical Mind.* Grand Rapids, MI: W. B. Eerdmans, 1994.

Novak, Michael. *The Joy of Sports: End Zones, Bases, Baskets, Balls, and the Consecration of the American Spirit.* New York: Basic Books, 1976.

Numbers, Ronald L. *The Creationists: From Scientific Creationism to Intelligent Design.* Cambridge, MA: Harvard University Press, 1992, 2006.

O'Guinn, Thomas C., and Russell W. Belk. "Heaven on Earth: Consumption at Heritage Village, USA." *Journal of Consumer Research* 16, no. 2 (September 1989): 227–38.

Orsi, Robert. "Everyday Miracles: The Study of Lived Religion." In *Lived Religion in America: Toward a History of Practice,* ed. David D. Hall, 3–21. Princeton, NJ: Princeton University Press, 1997.

Osborne, Catherine R. *American Catholics and the Church of Tomorrow: Building Churches for the Future, 1925–1975.* Chicago: University of Chicago Press, 2018.

Paine, Crispin. "Religious Theme Parks." *Material Religion* 12, no. 3 (2016): 402–3.

Pinsky, Mark. *The Gospel according to* The Simpsons*: The Spiritual Life of the World's Most Animated Family.* Louisville, KY: Westminster John Knox Press, 2001.

Plate, S. Brent. *Blasphemy: Art That Offends.* London: Black Dog, 2006.

Price, Joseph L., ed. *From Season to Season: Sports as American Religion.* Macon, GA: Mercer University Press, 2001.

Prince, Gregory O., and Wm. Robert Wright. *David O. McKay and the Rise of Modern Mormonism.* Salt Lake City: University of Utah Press, 2005.

Promey, Sally M., ed. *Sensational Religion: Sensory Cultures in Material Practice.* New Haven, CT: Yale University Press, 2014.

Rodash, Daniel. *Rapture Ready! Adventures in the Parallel Universe of Christian Pop Culture.* New York: Scribner, 2008.

Schmitt, Bill. *Words of Life: Celebrating 50 Years of the Hesburgh Library's Message, Mural, and Meaning.* Notre Dame, IN: University of Notre Dame Press, 2013.

Scholes, Jeffrey, and Raphael Sassower. *Religion and Sports in American Culture.* New York: Routledge, 2015.

Shepard, Charles E. *Forgiven: The Rise and Fall of Jim Bakker and the PTL Ministry.* New York: Atlantic Monthly Press, 1989.

Shipps, Jan. *Mormonism: The Story of a New Religious Tradition.* Urbana: University of Illinois Press, 1985.

Smith, Gerald L. K. *The Story of the Statue of* The Christ of the Ozarks. Eureka Springs, AR: Elna M. Smith Foundation, 1967.

Stevenson, Jill C. *Sensational Devotion: Evangelical Performance in Twenty-First-Century America.* Ann Arbor: University of Michigan Press, 2013.

Trillin, Calvin. "U.S. Journal: Eureka Springs, Ark., The Sacred Projects." *New Yorker,* July 26, 1969, 69–79.

Trollinger, Susan L., and William Vance Trollinger Jr. *Righting America at the Creation Museum.* Baltimore: Johns Hopkins University Press, 2017.

Upton, Dell. "Architectural History or Landscape History?" *Journal of Architectural Education* 44, no. 4 (August 1991): 195–99.

Wharton, Annabel Jane. *Selling Jerusalem: Relics: Replicas, Theme Parks.* Chicago: University of Chicago Press, 2006.

Wigger, John. *PTL: The Rise and Fall of Jim and Tammy Faye Bakker's Evangelical Empire.* New York: Oxford University Press, 2017.

Wilcox, Keith W. *The Washington DC Temple: A Light to the World: A History of Its Architectural Development.* Salt Lake City, Utah [?]: K. W. Wilcox, 1979, 1995.

Williams, Peter W. *Popular Religion in America: Symbolic Change and the Modernization Process in Historical Perspective.* Englewood Cliffs, NJ: Prentice-Hall, 1980.

Yanni, Carla. *Nature's Museums: Victorian Science and the Architecture of Display.* Baltimore: Johns Hopkins University Press, 1999.

# INDEX

*Italicized page numbers refer to illustrations.*

land USA proposed for, 85; Fort Heritage, 79, 83–84; Fort Hope, 83; fundraising for, 89–90, 93; Billy Graham childhood home rebuilt at, 84–85, 168n50; as heaven, 80; Heavenly Fudge Shoppe, 88; Heritage Gift Shoppe, 88; Heritage Grand Hotel, 75, 82, 84, *84,* 87, *87,* 89; Heritage Grand Ministry Center, 83, 87, *87;* Heritage Grand Towers, 82, 84, 89; Heritage House, 83, 109; Heritage Island water park, 73, 74, 81, 87, *87,* 89–90; Heritage Lake, 83, 87; Heritage USA West proposed for, 79; Heritage Village, 83; Heritage Village Church, 81, 82, 85; Heritage Village Church Academy, 83; Jerusalem amphitheater, 85; Kevin's House, 83, 168n41; King's Castle, 79, 167n26; Main Street shopping mall, 77, 79, 87–89, *87, 88,* 89, 109; Ministry Center proposed for, 78; Morningside Church, predecessor of, 109, 136; Noah's Toy Shoppe, 88; Old Jerusalem theme park proposed for, 72, 85, 95; Passion play, 85, 95; and Pentecostalism, 74, 89; petting zoo, 81, 86; as Protestant camp meeting ground, 83; and PTL, 75, 77, 82, 97; roller-skating rink, 81, 86–87; Royal Hair Design, 88; as ruin, 89; as sacred space, 80; School of Evangelism and Communications, 83; *The Simpsons* satire of, 4–5, 11, 71–72, 94–97, 108; tennis courts, 81, 87; Total Learning Center, 82; train, miniature, 73, 79, 86; Typhoon waterslide, 4, 8, 13, 75, 87, *87,* 90–93, *90, 92,* 96, 108, 111; university proposed for, 78; Upper Room Chapel, 83, 85, *86,* 89, 109; *The Wizard of Oz,* comparison to, 81; World Outreach Center, 83; world's fair, influence on, 78; Ye Old Bookstore, 88. *See also* Bakker, Jim; Bakker, Tammy Faye; Praise the Lord (PTL) network; theme park, evangelical
Heritage Village (North Carolina), 84; and Bruton Parish Church, 84
Hesburgh, Theodore M., 10, 17, 28–30, 32; and academic freedom, 29, 34, 158–59n59; "Statement on the Nature of the Contemporary Catholic University," 158–59n59; "Touchdown Jesus," denial of, 17, 39–40; UNAM, visit to, 33, 159n72; UNAM murals, response to, 33–35; as University of Notre Dame president, 17, 28–30. *See also* "Touchdown Jesus" (University of Notre Dame);

Universidad Nacional Autónoma de México (UNAM); University of Notre Dame (Indiana); *Word of Life, The* (mural; University of Notre Dame)
Hofstadter, Richard, 27, 29
Holy Land, re-creation of, 12, 72, 76–77, *76,* 85, 95, 141–42, *142,* 143, 146
Holy Land Experience (Florida), 77, 81–82, 109, 114, 170n79. *See also* theme park, evangelical
Holy Land USA (Connecticut), 76–77
Hough, Joseph C., 23
*Hustler Magazine v. Jerry Falwell,* 108
Huxley, Thomas, 120, 121
hyperreality, 80, 85

Immaculata College (Pennsylvania), women's basketball team, 24
*Inherit the Wind* (play/movie), 119
International Style, 34, 35, 104
Izenour, Steven, 58, 130

Jencks, Charles, 58
Jenkins, Henry, 7
Jerusalem, New. *See* City of God
Jerusalem, Old. *See* Holy Land, re-creation of
Jewish Anti-Defamation League of B'nai B'rith, 143
Jimmy Swaggart Bible College (Louisiana), 78
John, Gospel of, 16–17
John Paul II (pope), 4, 11, 24, 90, 92–93, 94
Johns Hopkins University (Maryland), 30
Johnson, Philip: and Crystal Cathedral, 166n23; and New York State Pavilion, 78, 98; and New York State Theater, 57
Jones, E. Fay, 137

*King of Kings* (statue; Ohio), 136, *137*
Koppel, Ted, 82, 169n59; and "Billion Dollar Pie," 108

*Language of Post-Modern Architecture, The* (Jencks), 58
Latter-day Saints, The Church of Jesus Christ of (LDS), 5, 10–11, 12, 47–48, 49, 51, 52, 53–54, 56, 58–59, 63, 64, 65, 150; and Book of Mormon, 47,

Midcentury: Architecture, Landscape, Urbanism, and Design